D0849812

Rational Acceptance and Purpose

RATIONAL ACCEPTANCE AND PURPOSE

An Outline of a Pragmatist Epistemology

D. S. Clarke, Jr.

ROWMAN & LITTLEFIELD PUBLISHERS, INC.

ROWMAN & LITTLEFIELD PUBLISHERS, INC.

Published in the United States of America in 1989
by Rowman & Littlefield Publishers, Inc.
81 Adams Drive, Totowa, New Jersey 07512

Copyright © 1989 by Rowman & Littlefield Publishers, Inc.

Library of Congress Cataloging-in-Publication Data

Clarke, D. S. (David S.), 1936–
    Rational acceptance and purpose: an outline of a
pragmatist epistemology / by D. S. Clarke, Jr.

    Bibliography: p. 137
    Includes indexes.
    ISBN 0–8476–7599–8.   ISBN 0–8476–7600–5 (pbk.)
    1. Knowledge, Theory
of.   2. Pragmatism.   I. Title.
    BD161.C56 1989   87–37680
    121—dc 19   CIP

5   4   3   2   1

Printed in the United States of America

To my daughters
Jessica and Kathy

Contents

viii   *Contents*

Preface

Pragmatism has enjoyed a welcome and overdue revival in recent years, with champions appearing in many quarters. They have, however, often lacked a clear understanding of its central theses and the difficulties confronting their alternative formulations. Nor have they been commonly stated these theses in a way that makes possible a clear contrast between pragmatism and the theories of knowledge and truth that have dominated philosophy in this century. This work is an attempt to state a version of pragmatism specific enough to make this contrast and, at the same time, defend itself against the principal criticisms levelled against alternative formulations. In general terms, pragmatism is understood here as a theory that claims that the standards used in justifying acceptance of a proposition as rational must include reference to individual or community purposes. The formulation of what is called the "Pragmatic Condition" in Chapter 4 is the central part of the version of this theory that I am advancing.

This is preceded by an introductory chapter and criticisms in Chapters 2 and 3 directed against theories of rational acceptance that exclude consideration of purposes. The first of these is a theory called "reliabilism," which states criteria for rational acceptance in terms of causal mechanisms that tend to produce true statements. The second, "probablism," states criteria appealing to numerical measures of justified belief called "logical probabilities." The exposition of the central claims of probabilism in Chapter 3 introduces technicalities which may not interest some readers. These occur principally in Sections 3.3 and 3.4, sections that can be skimmed through without losing the main thread of argument that is picked up in Section 3.5. The fifth and final chapter contrasts the theory developed in Chapter 4 with what I regard as erroneous versions first developed in the era of classical pragmatism through the writings of Peirce, James, and Dewey. My hope is to have been able to sift out from their seminal ideas a version of pragmatism that remains viable in present-day philosophy.

Most of this work was written while I was on sabbatical leave with my wife Sadako in Kyoto, Japan during the fall of 1986. I am grateful to our hosts, especially Seisaku Yamamoto of Kyoto University and Yoshinori Mitani, Ikken Nakayama, and Hachiro Tominaga of Kyoto Sangyo University, for helping to make our stay a very pleasant one. I am also grateful to my colleagues at Southern Illinois University, Mark Johnson, Thomas Mitchell, and Sudak Dharmardhikari, for helpful comments on an early manuscript draft. Mary Simmons of Rowman & Littlefield has added her deft improvements of a logician's tortured prose.

Carbondale, Illinois
January 16, 1988

Chapter 1

Introduction

This first chapter includes some preliminary conceptions and defines in general terms the basic issues of this work. I begin by outlining some comparative features of sentences of natural languages and of more primitive types of signs. The goal of a pragmatist epistemology is to describe the relationships between our purposes and the actions they guide, and the interpretation of increasingly complex sentences, including those of theoretical science. For this, the comparative study of different levels of signs provides a useful framework, since relationships between an agent's purposes and sign interpretation are more obvious for primitive signs than for more complex linguistic signs with their specialized functions. Of special interest is the acceptance of an utterance of a sentence at a given occasion as true. In Sections 1.2 and 1.3, some central features of acceptance are discussed, including its role in practical deliberation in guiding conduct and converting a descriptive sentence of theoretical science from the status of tentative hypothesis to being part of our background knowledge used in future inquiry. Finally, a preliminary statement is given of two contrasting views of how acceptance is to be justified. What we here label "cognitivism" claims that this justification must be stated by purely epistemic criteria in terms of logical relationships between propositions. In contrast, the view labelled "pragmatism" holds that criteria for evaluation must also include reference to the purposes of the inquirer and the community of which he or she is a part.

1.1. SENTENCES AND THEIR PRIMITIVE ANTECEDENTS

The most primitive signs, the evolutionary antecedents of all to follow, are what have been traditionally called natural signs as events in the environment of their interpreters. A person seeing lightning will expect thunder from the same direction and within a restricted interval. The lightning is then a natural sign whose significance or meaning is thunder as a type of event that is expected. It is expected within a certain spatial-temporal interval, or what we can term the sign's *referent occasion*. A sound of thunder following the lightning flash is recognized at this referent

1

occasion as a significate occurrence, an occurrence of the expected type of event, while for an absence of sound there would be a recognition of a significate non-occurrence. This latter recognition is normally followed either by a specification of the type of event that is discriminated in the future as having the significance of thunder—it is now not lightning-in-general, but lightning of a particular kind—or by a weakening of the expectation.

For adult humans interpretation of such natural events is normally overlaid by linguistic intermediaries; we perceive the events having significance as instances specified by linguistic descriptions and infer to other linguistic descriptions of the expected events. But for lower animals and prelinguistic infants it is reasonable to suppose that no such mediation is present, and the basic features of the account just given seem to be present.[1] Also, at this level expectation is combined with action in a way that requires signs to have a twofold significance. An odor or rustling of leaves for a deer in the forest may be signs of an approaching predator; to see the predator in the direction of the odor or sound would be to recognize a significate occurrence. But such signs also are signs for the deer of fleeing from the predator and thus signify actions in addition to types of environmental events. Similarly, the sight of a candle becomes a sign for the infant of intense heat, but it also signifies the action of hand withdrawal from a potential source of pain. In this way what we can term the *cognitive interpretation* of a sign as signifying a type of expected event is combined with its *dynamic interpretation* as signifying an action that secures a benefit or (as in the cases of the deer and child) avoids a harm.

Exactly how these two modes of interpretation are interrelated is difficult to determine. Certainly we can say that which events are discriminated by agents as objects of cognitive interpretation is determined by the purposes fulfilled by their signified actions. The deer's survival depends on escaping the predator. Hence, a certain odor or rustling sound is discriminated as a projectible sign with significance, while an indefinite variety of other sensed odors and sounds without links to the animal's purposes are ignored. But while the discrimination of a perceived event as a sign is influenced in this way by purposes, it is difficult to see how the recognition of significate occurrences or non-occurrences in the mode of cognitive interpretation could be similarly influenced. The deer may recognize a predator in the direction of the odor or sound, but this recognition does not itself seem to be a function of its desire to avoid the predator. Though the capacity to recognize significate occurrences or nonoccurrences and to modify sign types as having significance may have evolved through natural selection as a mechanism essential for survival, the exercise of this capacity on a given occasion seems to be only indirectly dependent on wants or aversions.

Signs of higher levels are characterized by increasingly wider extensions of referent occasions and by their use in communication situations. The simplest of communicated signs, those lacking internal subject-predicate structure, are *signals* such as warning cries, gestures, and single-word sentences such as 'Red' and 'Tree' as used by children in the early stages of language acquisition. Normally such signals are accompanied by gestures or the spatial orientation of the communicator that function to indicate the location of the referent occasion. I say 'Tree' to a child and point to a nearby location. Assuming the child has learned the meaning of the word through prior associations between utterances of it and the sight of particular trees, he will expect to see the tree at the indicated location. This referent occasion is now a place other than that at which I produce my utterance of 'Tree', and in this way the referent occasion is extended beyond that possible for natural signs. At the level of signals is also introduced the feature of conventionality. Signals may be nonconventional, as for a novel gesture picturing an action to be performed, e.g. when I indicate to another not speaking my language I want him to run by actually running myself. But typically they are conventional signs such as the word 'Tree' or the hand-up gesture used in most countries to give the command to stop. Conventional signals introduce 'truth' and 'falsity' as evaluative terms that are used to assess the utterances of the speaker. As we have seen, for a natural sign such as the flash of lightning recognition of a significate non-occurrence leads to a modification of the sign type having a given significance or to a weakening of future expectation. But if I say 'Tree' and another fails to see a tree at the indicated location, he would reject what I have said as false and perhaps change his assessment of me as a reliable informant. The sign type 'Tree' remains itself fixed by the conventions of the English language, a type of permanence indispensable for effective communication.

Sentences as combinations of subject and predicate terms introduce still further extensions of the referent occasion. To use a sentence such as 'Jones is tall', with the proper name 'Jones' as subject and 'is tall' as predicate, is to inform the hearer that whenever or wherever the individual Jones is actually identified it can be expected that he will have the attribute of being tall. The referent occasion as the time and place of such identification is thus indefinitely extended beyond the immediate environment to remote locations. At the level of sentences, specialization of functions is also introduced. A warning cry as signal can be both a sign of an approaching predator and of the action of fleeing to escape. But the linguistic level allows a distinction between the indicative sentence 'Jones is tall' used to describe and imperative sentences such as 'Hit the ball' or 'Jump over the fence' in which 'the ball' and 'the fence' function as subjects referring to objects that serve to orient the actions prescribed by the predicates 'hit' and 'jump over'. It is this specialization of function that promotes the mistaken philosophic view that the interpretation of descriptive sentences in the indicative mood can be divorced from actions and the purposes they fulfill.

That this interpretation is inextricably linked to action can be seen for even the simplest forms of singular descriptive sentences. We noted how subjects of such sentences extend the referent occasion by referring to objects remote from the time and place at which the sentence is being used. The role of these subjects can be regarded as serving what Charles Peirce termed "precepts," directing the hearer how to proceed in locating and identifying the object.[2] To say, for example, 'The old man living by the bridge is rich' is to direct the hearer to go next to the bridge and look for someone old in order to identify the man who is said to be wealthy. For a proper name such as 'Jones' in 'Jones is tall', there will be associated descriptive phrases, e.g. 'My next door neighbor living in the large house', which express the meaning of the name and provide similar directives. Of course, in normal communication we do not usually actually follow such directions, but instead accept the information conveyed and act in accordance with it. Suppose I were to be driving on a road and were stopped by a policeman who tells me 'The bridge two miles ahead has collapsed on this road'. I would act on this information and make a detour rather than drive the two miles to check on the accuracy of what I have been told. But I could make this check, and the decision to act now on the policeman's report is, in effect, a decision not to follow the guidelines provided by the sentence's subject. The potential action of identification is thus always in the background of the interpretation of such a descriptive sentence.

So far we have been considering only isolated sentences. The next level of sign is occupied by combinations of sentences forming blocks of *discourse* in the forms of conversation, narration, directives, inferences with premises and conclusion, etc.—forms that become more complex as writing is introduced as a means of communication. At this level sentences become interrelated, and what is called a proposition must be introduced to stand for the common content expressed by sentences within a given discourse. For example, consider the modus ponens deductive inference 'If Harry is married to Alice, he is the father of Roderick; Alice is married to Harry; hence, Harry is Roderick's father'. The validity of this inference depends on the pairs of sentences 'Harry is married to Alice'and 'Alice is married to Harry' being in some sense identical, and 'He is the father of Roderick' and 'Harry is Roderick's father' also having a common content. The identical contents they express are the propositions that preserve the relations essential for the validity of the inference. When we speak of "accepting a proposition as true," we are invariably referring to the acceptance of an utterance or inscription as it occurs within such a discursive context.

Forms of discourse tend to have increasingly specialized functions as used by differing social groups with special training in their use. The language of theoretical science constitutes a highly general framework of discourse in which the different special sciences—physics, chemistry, biology, psychology—and their various branches have their own special terminology for describing their special domains of study. Characteristic of these forms of discourse is the presence of complex inferential relationships between propositions expressed by constituent sentences. Three main types of sentences occur as the premisses and conclusions of these inferences.

(1) *Singular Descriptions*. In the context of scientific inquiry these are often what are called "observation sentences" describing initial conditions and outcomes of experimental tests, e.g. 'This is a robin's egg', 'This egg is blue', 'The pointer on this instrument is aligned at 20', 'This piece of metal weighs 20 grams', 'This litmus paper is immersed in water', 'This paper has turned red', 'There is a .5 centimeter long streak on this photograph', 'A muon particle was emitted by this collision'. But singular descriptions can also function as hypotheses which themselves must be subject to observational testing, as for 'The earth has a radius of 6,378 kilometers' or 'Our galaxy contains approximately 100 billion stars'.

(2) *Empirical generalizations*. There are three principal forms of empirical generalizations:

(a) *Attribute ascriptions*. These ascribe an attribute to a kind of object. They can be uniform generalizations, e.g. 'All robin eggs are blue' and 'All mammals have brains', or statistical generalizations such as 'The probability of a man being left handed is .25'.

(b) *Causal generalizations*. These state causal relations between two events, and can also be uniform or statistical, e.g. 'Immersing litmus paper in acid causes it to turn red', 'The probability of humans being infected by rabies when bitten by dogs is .14'.

(c) *Functional correlations*. These quantitative generalizations state *how much* of a measurable degree of one variable (the dependent variable) varies with a measurable degree of variation of one or more other variables (the independent variables). The general form is $y = f(x_1, x_2, \ldots, x_n)$, with y the dependent variable and $x_1, x_2, \ldots, x_n$ the n number of independent variables. Well-known examples include: 'For any metal, its displacement (D) is directly proportional to the force (F) exerted on it', or '$D = kF$' (Hooke's law), where k is a constant varying with the type of metal; 'For any freely falling body, the distance traveled (s) is directly proportional to the square of the time interval (t), or '$s = 16t^2$' (Galileo's law of acceleration); and 'For any ideal gas, the pressure exerted by a gas on the sides of a container (P) is directly proportional to the temperature (T) and inversely proportional to the volume (V)' or 'P

$= kT/V'$ (the ideal gas law). The subject terms of these correlations are respectively the terms 'metal', 'freely falling body', and 'ideal gas' referring to the types of objects to which the correlations apply.

(3) *Theories*. These are combinations of sentences referring to a wide domain of objects from which more specific empirical generalizations of the kind just listed can be deductively inferred and thus explained. The fundamental theories of physics such as Einstein's gravitational theory and quantum mechanics have as their subjects the term 'material thing' referring to the widest possible domain of objects. In physics, theories typically take the form of combinations of functional correlations stated as differential equations from which specific empirical functional correlations are deductively derived as solutions. In this derivation, information about the special features referred to by the generalizations is employed.

In addition to this deductive inferential relation, two other relationships between the sentences just listed are topics of later discussions. Observation sentences serve as the premises from which empirical generalizations as conclusions are inferred within inductive inferences. Thus, we may infer from the observation sentences 'This robin egg is blue', 'This other robin egg is blue', and 'These others are too' to the universal attribute ascription 'All robin eggs are blue' or from 'This litmus paper has been immersed in acid and turned red' and 'Immersing these others has had the same result' to the causal generalization 'Immersing litmus paper in acid causes it to turn red'. These inferences and the procedural rules governing the selection of their premises will be discussed in Section 3.1. The other relationship of interest to us is that between empirical generalizations and theories on the one hand and observation sentences on the other in which the results of experimental tests are interpreted. This will be discussed briefly when we turn to forms of background knowledge in Section 3.3 of this chapter.

In his *Treatise*[3] Hume writes of the "causal reasoning" of animals, and philosophers since have compared animal learning to inductive inferences from observation sentences to generalizations. Thus, Quine and Ullian write:

> Essentially it [induction] is just a matter of learning from experience what to expect; and everyone is at it continually. Other animals are at it too in learning what to avoid and where to go for food and water. All such learning...depends on a prior tendency to notice certain traits and so to single them out for projection rather than others.[4]

Given the enormous differences between the interpretation of natural signs and making inferences between sentences as conventional linguistic signs this comparison is more misleading than helpful. There is undoubtedly some analogy between a child's learning the meaning of observational terms such as 'red', 'green', 'tree', and 'book', and a lower animal's learning to interpret an odor as a sign of a food source to be sought after. But once the terms have been learned as entrenched items of the lexicon of our language, the child goes on to combine them to form sentences with subjects and predicates, and then acquires the capacity to infer from some sentence to others. It is at this stage that such significantly new features of interpretation are introduced as to render any analogy to animal learning tenuous at best.

Nevertheless, a pragmatic view of inquiry of the kind defended here insists on a role for human purposes in inductive reasoning that does bear an analogy to the role of wants and aversions in animal learning. The exact nature of this analogy can only be determined after tracing the special characteristics of descriptive language as used in ordinary communication situations and in the more specialized forms of scientific inquiry.

1.2 PRACTICAL INFERENCES AND ACCEPTANCE

We humans rarely guide our actions by interpreting natural events in our environment. Instead, they are guided by what we call *practical reasoning*, and the form of reasoning usually employed is one where we infer from the premisses to the conclusion of a *practical inference* requiring a given action. It is by examining features of the use of such practical inferences that we see most clearly the relationships between our purpose-directed actions and information conveyed by descriptive language in everyday life.

One principal form of inference used in practical deliberation contains a premiss expressing the want of the agent for a state of affairs that we alternatively refer to as his *purpose*, his *end*, or that in which he has an *interest*. There are in addition two descriptive premisses, one stating that an action we call the *means* to this end must be performed if a circumstance beyond his control were to obtain, the other that this circumstance does in fact obtain.[5] Suppose, for example, that I want to stay warm while outdoors this winter and accept as a matter of fact that if this winter is a cold one I must buy a coat to stay warm and that the winter will be cold. Then I would infer that I should buy a coat. The inference used is thus:

I want to keep warm this winter
Only if I buy a coat will I stay warm if this winter is cold
It will be cold this winter
_____

Therefore, I ought to buy a coat

The inference's general form is

I want E
My doing M is a necessary condition for E if C
C will obtain
==
I ought to do M

where E is the end, M the means to this end, and C the circumstance. The double lines separating the premises from the conclusion indicate that the inference is a nondeductive one with a defeasible conclusion, which could be rejected as false if the premises fail to express all the relevant wants and aversions of the agent. The cost of buying a coat, for example, may be high for me, or require my diverting funds from other desired purchases, and I may prefer to forego keeping warm rather than incur these costs. In situations like this where the cost of M outweighs the benefit to the agent he would not accept the conclusion.

Assuming the agent still prefers E after weighing the various costs of the means M against his want for E, however, his acceptance of the descriptive second and third premises would seem to commit him to accepting the conclusion. To refuse to accept the conclusion's requirement indicates that the agent has not really accepted the descriptive premises given the background of his wanting E after weighing M's costs.[6] He may *say* to another that he must buy the coat to stay warm and that it will be a cold winter, but he has not really accepted these premises if the commitment to buying the coat is not made, a commitment that is a requirement of practical rationality.

Three features of these inferences are worth noting. The first is that there is a difference in form between their two descriptive, fact-stating premises. The third premiss is a categorical description of a state of affairs, e.g. that next winter will be cold, that the road ahead is blocked. The second premiss is, in contrast, a counterfactual conditional that can be based in complex ways on causal and functional generalizations. It states, in effect, that only if I *were* to do M would E be a consequence if the circumstance C *were* to obtain. In other versions of practical inferences this second premiss can state that M is sufficient for E, that if M were performed E would follow as consequence. Often we learn directly through personal experience or practical training by others how our actions can bring about desired consequences. But we can also base our acceptance of this type of descriptive premise on empirical generalizations that initially have no practical import. To accept the generalization stating that lowering the of temperature of water below 32° Fahrenheit causes it to freeze is to also accept a means-end sentence that can be deductively inferred from it, e.g. that if I were to lower the temperature of this container of water I would make it freeze. Similarly, to accept as functional correlation Archimedes' law of levers is to accept a means-end sentence stating that my applying X quantity of force to the end of a lever at distance D from a fulcrum is necessary and sufficient for lifting an object of weight Y at a distance D' from it.

Next, it is important to see that the basic logical relationships between premises and conclusion remain unchanged if one or both of the descriptive premises state probabilities. Suppose I were to accept as true the more qualified sentence 'It is likely to be a cold winter' or (as conveyed by a long-range forecast) 'It will be cold with a probability of .7'. Then I could still infer 'I ought to buy a coat', provided my desire for warmth outweighs my aversion to the cost as combined with my estimate as to how likely it will be necessary to incur it. Obviously, the lower the probability of the circumstance, the less likely will the desire for the end outweigh for me the aversion to the cost of the means. Such combinations of probabilities with preferences are usually discussed in forms of practical inferences in which alternative means to an end are stated. The calculation of the "expected utilities" of alternative means is the topic of decision theory and will be outlined in Chapter 4.

Finally, we must recognize that the basic inferential relationships are drastically altered if we replace the descriptive premises by expressions of belief. To express a belief in a proposition, as opposed to asserting it, is typically to qualify one's assertion, to indicate some hesitancy, and to refuse to make a total endorsement of it. To choose to say 'I believe that it is raining' instead of simply saying 'It is raining' is to add a qualification that serves to release us from responsibility if the proposition proves to be false. Beliefs admit of degrees, ranging from a "weak" belief that it is more likely that a proposition is true than false to a "strong" belief that approaches virtual certainty. But even to say 'I strongly believe that it is raining' is to indicate some hesitancy that falls short of endorsement. These features of our use of 'believe' have the effect of making belief sentences unacceptable substitutes for the unqualified descriptive premisses used in practical inferences. To say only 'I believe my doing M is necessary for E' or 'I believe that C' in no way commits the agent to accepting the normative requirement 'I ought to do M', given the background of wants and preferences we have been assuming. Nor does any other normative requirement seem to follow. The belief sentences are expressing only the subjective beliefs of the agent, and these may in themselves be quite irrational. Clearly, no requirement for action can be inferred from what are merely subjective attitudes.

This situation is changed if the beliefs are not those which the agent *happens* to hold but are instead *rational* beliefs, beliefs that he holds relative to the best available evidence. Thus, I may not simply believe that next winter will be cold, a belief that may be based only on an intuitive guess, but hold this belief after a thorough research of the relevant weather statistics, patterns of climatic change, etc. But even for beliefs that we can label as "rational," the strongest normative conclusion we seem to be able to infer is that it is rational to perform the necessary means to the desired end. We thus have the inference,

I want E
I rationally believe that my doing M is necessary for E if C
I rationally believe that C
====
It is rational for me to do M.

The conclusion of this inference would seem to fall short of the unqualified commitment to action that attends acceptance of an 'ought' conclusion. There seems to be no inconsistency in a person saying 'It is rational for me to do M, but I am not going to do M', as someone may realize a certain horse is a hopeless choice, but for sentimental reasons still bet on him to win a race. Indeed, we often approve of those who disregard what is regarded as the "reasonable" thing to do. But an 'ought' conclusion allows no such escape; it is inconsistent to say 'I ought to do M, but I won't'. Through weakness of will the action M may not actually be performed, but the commitment to perform it is nevertheless made once the 'ought' conclusion is accepted.[7]

Often the descriptive premises of a practical inference are based on other accepted descriptions and function as what Ullman-Margalit terms *presumptions* relative to these other descriptions.[8] A presumption is not directly confirmed relative to one's own experience, but is accepted without further questioning relative to what is, or at least could be, so confirmed. The most common presumptions are those descriptions provided through the testimony of others. The policeman tells me that the road ahead is blocked by a collapsed bridge; I accept what he tells me as true and take a detour. The weather forecaster tells me that next winter will be cold, or that there is a .7 probability of it being cold; I use his report as a presumptive premise in a practical inference of the kind given above. Given the elaborate social dependencies that have evolved, we must and we do trust others to provide reliable information. The fact that someone asserts to us with apparent sincerity the proposition p usually constitutes for us sufficient grounds for our assenting to or accepting p as true. The proposition p then becomes a potential presumptive premise in a practical inference. Of course, witnesses can prove to be unreliable, and there are occasions when we would want to check on the testimony of others. Also, we tend to trust those in positions of special authority or responsibility, the policeman or the trained weather forecaster, more than those we randomly meet. Nevertheless, in the absence of grounds for doubt, we do bestow this trust and use the assertions of others as descriptive premises from which to infer to what we should do.

So far we have been discussing only the acceptance of descriptive sentences in the context of practical inferences used by all of us in everyday life. When we turn to scientific inquiry as the activity of a specialized profession, acceptance takes on different forms. Within this inquiry we can distinguish two distinct stages. In the first, a hypothesis is proposed as a possible description of some state of affairs, often as an alternative to other competing hypotheses. It is then subject to experimental testing in order to either confirm it as a true description or falsify it in preparation for the consideration of other alternatives. In the second stage, the hypothesis is accepted as true or rejected as false. Corresponding to these stages we can distinguish two types of acceptance. To initiate a series of tests of a hypothesis a decision must be made that the hypothesis is a plausible one, that it deserves consideration as a viable candidate among alternatives.[9] Some hypotheses never pass this initial screening and fail to be given further consideration. We can refer to the decision to proceed with testing of a given hypothesis *h* as the *provisional acceptance* of *h*. In contrast to this initial acceptance, there is what we can refer to as the *terminal acceptance* of *h* or its negation (the rejection of *h* as false) on the basis of the results of observational testing.[10] In certain intractable areas of scientific inquiry, years or even decades can separate the two decisions.

Of the two forms, provisional acceptance can be most easily linked to action. To provisionally accept a hypothesis is simply to decide to perform a series of tests, and these tests involve actions such as selecting objects, isolating causal factors, measuring values of variables, and constructing instruments of measurement, depending on the nature of the hypothesis under consideration. But the link between terminal acceptance and subsequent actions is more difficult to make. In applied science, of course, terminal acceptance is directly related to actions in the manner just outlined for practical deliberation. To accept as true after testing the hypothesis that a drug *Z* has no harmful side-effects is to enable the inference to the conclusion of a practical inference that *Z* ought to be administered to the general public. But in theoretical science a given hypothesis may have no direct relation to specific actions, at least not at the time of its terminal acceptance, and when applications are found they may be diverse and serve many purposes. Thus, Hubbel's hypothesis of the receding galaxies had, after its acceptance, no practical applications and will have none in the foreseeable future, while acceptance of Watson and Crick's double helix model of the DNA molecule has lead to a wide variety of applications in medicine and in the development of new strains of organisms.

If there is a relationship between terminal acceptance in the theoretical sciences and our purposes and actions, it is thus an indirect and complex one, certainly more complex than that for the descriptive premises in a practical inference. To begin to understand this relationship first requires a closer examination of the nature of terminal acceptance and of its effects on future inquiry. This is done in the next section. In the discussion that follows, 'acceptance' should always be understood to mean terminal acceptance; if provisional acceptance is intended, it will be specifically indicated.

1.3 BACKGROUND KNOWLEDGE

By the *background knowledge* of a person (or community of inquirers) we shall understand that set of propositions assumed to be true and whose assumption guides inquiry. Our background knowledge thus consists of those "facts" taken for granted as we pose questions and attempt to answer them. These assumptions may include many that we cannot explicitly formulate. The classical concept of knowledge (discussed in the next chapter) requires that in order for a person to be said to know a proposition, it must be true. The propositions making up what we are terming background knowledge may fail to conform to this classical requirement. Some of the members of our set of assumptions may, in fact, be false, and subsequent evidence may require us to acknowledge this. But these propositions *function* for us *as if* they were true, as not open to serious doubt, and in this capacity guide our inquiry.

In two important passages in *On Certainty*[11] Wittgenstein refers to the role in inquiry of certain propositions isolated from doubt. In the first he writes of the transition of a descriptive sentence from the status of a hypothesis to its directing subsequent inquiry.

Can't an assertoric sentence, which was capable of functioning as an hypothesis, also be used as a foundation for research and action? I.e. can't it simply be isolated from doubt, though not according to any explicit rule? It simply gets assumed as a truism, never called in question, perhaps not even formulated.

In a second passage he refers to the set of such assumed "truisms" as constituting a "system" within which inferential inquiry takes place.

All testing, all confirmation and disconfirmation of a hypothesis takes place already within a system. And this system is not a more or less arbitrary and doubtful point of departure, as the element in which arguments have their life.

What we are calling the "background knowledge" of a person or community constitutes such a system.[12]

To accept a hypothesis as true within the context of scientific inquiry is to convert it from its provisional status as subject to testing to what now is no longer in question and which functions to guide actions taken in future inquiry. This relation between acceptance and transition to inclusion in background knowledge is a conceptual relation analogous to that between acceptance and commitment to action in practical deliberation. Inclusion in the background is a logical result of acceptance, not a contingent consequence. If a given hypothesis does not actually function as an assumption guiding inquiry, then a person may *say* he accepts it as true, but he has not really accepted the hypothesis. It still has for him provisional status.

Background knowledge takes many forms. Some of the more important of them are now listed.

Predication and Meaning Transference

Suppose someone tells me 'Jones is an old man who is bald', referring to someone whom I have heard of but never met. Suppose also that I trust my informant as reliable and accept his remark as being true. Then the meaning of the terms 'old', 'man', and 'bald' in the predicate of his sentence will tend to be transferred to its subject 'Jones'. If I were later faced with the task of picking out Jones from a group of people, I would use the attributes of old age, being a man, and being bald as criteria for identifying him. In this way acceptance of an utterance of a sentence as true changes the nature of the precept conveyed by the subject and commits us to a course of action in identifying its referent. Of course, what my informant told me about Jones may be mistaken; indeed, everything I, or even the community of which I am a part, may have accepted about Jones may prove later to be mistaken, and none of the attributes I use for identification may actually be true of him.[13] In such cases correction of the mistake normally leads to accepting sentences with different predicates ascribed to the subject. This in turn leads to a change of the meaning of this subject and a commitment to applying novel criteria for identification.

This meaning transference from the predicate of an accepted sentence is also characteristic of ascriptive generalizations established in scientific inquiry. At an early stage in the history of chemistry and after a period of testing it as a hypothesis, the sentence 'Alcohol boils at 78.3°C' describing the boiling point of alcohol was accepted by the scientific community as true. At the time of acceptance qualitative criteria such as its being a clear bright liquid with a unique odor and viscosity were employed in identifying a given substance as alcohol. But after the acceptance of the boiling point hypothesis the meaning of its predicate became transferred to its subject 'alcohol' and hence part of the term's identifying criteria; to be alcohol is now to boil at 78.3°C. This criterion was then used in identifying instances of alcohol in order to test hypotheses ascribing different attributes. In general, let 'All S is P_1', 'All S is P_2', . . . ,'All S is P_n' be n number of hypotheses which are generalizations with subject S and predicates $P_1, P_2, \ldots, P_n$. To accept these n hypotheses as true is for the predicates $P_1, P_2, \ldots, P_n$ to now express criteria for an object being an S. After acceptance these criteria are used in identifying Ss in order to test a further hypothesis 'All S is P_{n+1}'. Before its acceptance a given hypothesis 'All S is P_k' is in Kant's terminology a "synthetic a posteriori" sentence, one whose predicate is not "included" in the subject and which is empirically testable. After acceptance when P_k becomes a criterion for identifying an S, the same sentence becomes an "analytic" sentence, one where the predicate is "included" in S as expressing one of its identifying criteria. But it is not (as Kant held) a necessarily true sentence. The fact that the scientific community has accepted an attribute expressed by a given P_k as holding of a certain S is no guarantee that at some later time it will not discover that P_k does not hold and reject 'All S is P_k' as false.[14]

One form that background knowledge takes in scientific inquiry, then, results from the transference of the meaning of predicates of accepted sentences to their subjects. To accept these sentences is to commit oneself to applying the criteria for identification that have been transferred.

Interpretation of Observation Sentences

A second form of background knowledge, one closely related to the first, is employed in the interpretation of observation sentences. With the exception of such reports as 'This looks blue' or 'That looks blurred to me', every observation sentence can be regarded as presupposing for its interpretation previously accepted sentences. Thus, in weighing an object a person may report 'The pointer on this scale is pointing at 12'. But the person may know (that is, take for granted what has been agreed upon) that the scale is subdivided into units of weight as measured in grams and that Hooke's law $F = kD$ together with the construction of the weighing instrument establishes a proportionality between the weight of the object and the displacement of the pointer on the scale. He or she will then interpret this sentence as being synonymous with 'This object weighs 12 grams'. More complex forms of interpretation can be found where accepted theories are presupposed. An outcome of an experiment can be reported as 'There is a streak .25 centimeters long on this photographic plate'. However, by the trained physicist the sentence may be interpreted as meaning 'This particle collision produced a muon as one of its effects'. The interpretation is based on acceptance of theories in nuclear physics as applied to the instruments and circumstances of the experiment.[15] To accept the theories is to give a certain interpretive description of what is observed.

Simpler examples of the role of background knowledge can be derived from the account of meaning transference given above. Suppose someone were to report 'The alcohol in this container weighs 100 grams'. Such a report would be based on the acceptance of descriptions of alcohol whose predicates have become criteria for identification, e.g. 'boils at 78.3°C', for these criteria will be used in identifying the liquid in the container as what is referred to by 'alcohol'. In this manner, every observation sentence with a noun subject is asserted relative to background knowledge, since every such subject will express criteria gained by transfer that will be used in identifying the instance being described.

Observation sentences are used in testing empirical generalizations and theories. As has been emphasized by many philosophers of science, the fact that the manner of formulation of these observation sentences is itself based on the acceptance of hypotheses that may later be reversed introduces an element of fallibility in every experimental test. An experiment may at first be regarded as falsifying a given hypothesis or being crucial in deciding between two or more alternatives. But if one of the assumptions employed in interpreting and describing it is itself rejected as false, the test may be thrown out as inconclusive. Though the correction of such mistakes often eventually proves useful, valuable time and resources expended in performing the experiment may have been wasted.

Inferential Assumptions

Those assumptions enabling the derivation of deductive consequences from hypotheses also affect the validity of an experimental test. Provisional acceptance is typically accorded a theory when accepted empirical generalizations or "laws" can be deductively inferred from it. But such a derivation almost invariably requires using what we accept as "facts" about the restricted domain of objects to which the empirical generalizations are applied. Thus, Newton's theory of gravitation gained its initial plausibility in part because from it Galileo's law of constant acceleration for freely falling bodies could be derived. But in order to derive the law from the theory it had to be assumed that the difference between the radius of the earth and the distance of a falling body from the earth's center is negligible. Background knowledge used in derivations include propositions explaining the deviation of observed results from those predicted from the ideal conditions postulated by a theory. If assumptions used in derivations prove mistaken, the test of the theory will often fail to be decisive. A consequence C may be derived from a theory T plus assumptions $A_1, A_2, \ldots, A_n$, and an experiment may show that C failed to occur as predicted. By modus tollens, we can then infer that either T or one of $A_1, A_2, \ldots, A_n$ is false. If $A_1, A_2, \ldots, A_n$ are all in fact true, we would have falsified T. But if one of them were to be later rejected, this would then force a reconsideration of the result of the test.

Experimental Design

In the preliminary stages of investigation of a given range of phenomena scientists must make a number of decisions regarding the exact formulations of the questions to be posed, the alternative hypotheses to be provisionally accepted as viable, possible answers, and procedures to be followed in the selection of relevant evidence and construction of instruments. These decisions all fall under the general heading of the *experimental design* of a given program of research. There are three main aspects to experimental design.

(1) Formulation of questions. Every accepted answer to a question itself serves as the potential basis for asking new questions. The answer is commonly referred to as the *presupposition* for the new question. For example, having answered the question 'What is the cause of cancer?' by 'A virus causes cancer', we proceed to ask 'What form of virus causes *this* kind of cancer?' Suppose the answer that is accepted to the latter is of the form 'Virus of type Y is the cause of cancer of type Z'. Then we can proceed to ask 'How does Y function to cause Z?' Successive answers thus generate successively more precise questions that delimit the outlines of a new inquiry. If the presupposition of a given question proves later to have been mistaken, e.g. if cancer has some cause other than a virus, then attempts to answer the question will likely to be fruitless and involve expenditures of wasted resources. How questions also generate a range of alternative answers and hence determine the information content of any of them will be a topic we will turn to below in Section 4.4.

(2) Provisional acceptance. In the previous section we noted the distinction between the provisional acceptance of a hypothesis as a subject for testing and its terminal acceptance in which it makes the transition to inclusion in our background knowledge. Provisional acceptance of a given hypothesis h_k is a decision to include it among the n alternative hypotheses $h_1, h_2, \ldots, h_n$ regarded as viable possible answers to the question being posed. Whether h_k is to be included will normally be determined relative to background assumptions.[16] That virus Y is the cause of cancer Z may be *logically* possible, but other information we take for granted may exclude it as a cause that we are willing to invest time and resources in considering it as a serious candidate. The effect of such exclusions is to greatly simplify the course of research, for the number of possible explanations of a given phenomenon is normally far greater than those we judge to be viable candidates. But there is again the risk that a background assumption used in making exclusions may later be rejected as false. This may delay obtaining an answer to the question posed and result in wasted effort.

(3) Judging relevance. Closely related to the exclusion of possible hypotheses is the use of background assumptions to make decisions about the relevancy of evidence. Such decisions are especially important where there is considerable variability within the objects being studied, as in biology, psychology, and sociology. Suppose an investigator is studying the mating behavior of a certain species of fish. Then background information will direct him or her to regard the sex, age, and perhaps geographical location of the fish as relevant to such behavior and to vary them among the sample selected as evidence. This same information may enable him to ignore random variations in coloration or size as irrelevant. Similar decisions for sample selection are made in studying the effects of drugs administered to primates or humans, or the voting preferences of the adults of a given country. As for hypothesis exclusion, the effect of applying background assumptions here is to enable economy of effort by limiting to manageable proportions the evidence from which generalizations are to be inductively inferred. But there is again the risk that a mistaken assumption will invalidate the results of inquiry.

(4) Construction of instruments. Finally, an investigator will often be forced to invent and have constructed an instrument to be used in conducting a specific experimental test. Construction of this instrument will require applying information acquired from some previously accepted generalization or theory, as Hooke's law is presupposed in constructing a spring weighing device. As we have seen, the interpretation of the recordings of the instruments will make use of this same information.

The forms of background knowledge just reviewed have been extensively discussed by philosophers of science. My purpose here has been to briefly indicate how acceptance of a hypothesis in the context of theoretical science does require commitment to actions. These actions do not fulfill specific personal or social goals, as in everyday practical deliberation or applied science. Instead, they are actions undertaken in future inquiry that are guided by the hypothesis after it becomes a background assumption. As we have seen, a mistaken assumption brings with it the cost of wasting the time, resources, and energy invested in performing these actions. In Chapter 4 we shall discuss in more detail some of the philosophic implications of these features of acceptance in theoretical inquiry.

1.4 COGNITIVISM AND PRAGMATISM

So far I have given a largely descriptive account of some general features of our use of language, practical inferences, and background assumptions. Its main outlines, if not all details, would be agreed to, I think, by nearly all philosophers. The principal controversies begin when we attempt to draw conclusions from these features regarding the central normative problem related to our use and interpretation of descriptive language. This is the problem of specifying the evaluative criteria we employ in assessing whether or not an individual or a community of inquirers should or should not accept a given proposition as true on a certain occasion. Alternatively, it is the problem of specifying criteria for determining whether or not acceptance is *rational* or *justified*.

This is, of course, a quite different problem from that of determining whether or not a proposition is true. The Chief of Police of a town may accept as true the proposition that Smith murdered Jones and bring Smith to trial. Suppose that during the trial new evidence comes to light that clearly shows that Smith is innocent, that someone who looked like Smith committed the murder. The proposition accepted by the Chief was then proven to be false. Still, we could judge that he was originally justified in accepting the proposition: he had carefully considered the evidence available at the time; the evidence conclusively established Smith's guilt; the new evidence brought to light could not have reasonably been foreseen. Similarly, the fact that Smith is later proven to have been guilty is not in itself sufficient to establish that the Chief was rational in originally accepting the proposition. His evidence at the earlier time may have been scanty; he may have reached his conclusion hastily because of some bias against Smith. The question of rational acceptance is in this way independent of the question of truth.

How is rational acceptance to be determined? To this two general theories have been proposed as answers. I offer now a preliminary sketch of these alternatives. I also indicate some individual philosophers from philosophy's past and present who can be associated with the two theories. But the association should be regarded as a loose one, and I do not want to claim that an individual philosopher who endorses one of the claims listed under one of these theories must therefore endorse them all, or that a philosopher could not consistently develop a modified theory that combines claims within both theories. Indeed, the version I shall be advocating makes some key concessions to some arguments made in support of the opposing theory. What we have instead is a loose constellation of claims that have been associated in the history of philosophy. The detailed formulation and assessment of them is the task of later chapters.

Cognitivism

By *cognitivism*[17] we shall understand the theory that holds acceptance of a proposition as true in the context of scientific inquiry is to be evaluated as rational if and only if it satisfies what I shall refer to as *purely epistemic criteria*. Such criteria include only those requiring acceptance to conform to science's aim of attaining the truth free of the biases and distortions of our interests and purposes. For a given proposition to be true, according to this theory, it must correspond to an independent state of affairs in nature. Cognitivism holds that acceptance is justified so far as there is conformity to rules that if followed in the long run would insure such correspondence. For most advocates of cognitivism these rules include both the inductive rules by which we infer from observation sentences to empirical generalizations and the procedural rules governing our selection of evidence to be used as premises in inductive inferences.

Others in the cognitivist tradition have denied that conformity to such rules is sufficient to justify acceptance. These philosophers permit acceptance only for those scientific conclusions of which we can be justifiably certain. Such certainty could only be attained if we were able to deductively infer them from premises that are themselves certain or self-evident. Since no reasoning to an empirical hypothesis conforms to this ideal, they deny that we can ever be justified in accepting any hypothesis. The best we can do is to confer provisional acceptance and employ a given hypothesis as a basis for practical actions. This is the version of cognitivism known as skepticism. When it becomes our topic in Section 2.2 we shall see that it fails to adequately account for the features of scientific inquiry described in the previous section. As an alternative to skepticism some philosophers in the cognitivist tradition have also attempted to formulate rules of acceptance that license our acceptance or rejection of a given hypothesis relative to either what is called its "logical probability" or its survival of attempts to falsify it. What are referred to as *probabilism* and *falsificationism* are the theories formulating these rules of acceptance. Probabilism is discussed in some detail in the last two sections of Chapter 3, while falsificationism is more briefly sketched in this chapter's first and final sections.

Whether of the skeptical or nonskeptical variety, all forms of cognitivism make a sharp distinction between acceptance within the context of practical deliberation and acceptance in theoretical science. Though he is known as the founder of American pragmatism, Peirce eloquently defended the importance of distinguishing the aims of scientific inquiry from aims of inquiry directed towards solving practical problems.

> The value of *Facts* to it [science], lies only in this, that they belong to Nature; and Nature is something great, and beautiful, and sacred, and eternal, and real—the object of its worship and its aspiration. It therein takes an entirely different attitude toward facts from that which Practice takes. . . . Science, when it comes to understand itself, regards facts as merely the vehicle of eternal truth, while for Practice they remain obstacles which it has to turn, the enemy of which it is determined to get the better. Science feeling that there is an arbitrary element in its theories, still continues its studies, confident that so it will gradually become more and more purified from the dross of subjectivity; but practice requires something to go upon, and it will

be no consolation to it to know that it is on the path to objective truth—the actual truth it must have, or when it cannot attain certainty must at least have high probability, that is, must know that, though a few of its ventures may fail, the bulk of them will succeed. Hence the hypothesis which answers the purpose of theory may be perfectly worthless for art. . . . belief is the willingness to risk a great deal upon a proposition. But this belief is no concern of science, which has nothing at stake on any temporal venture but is in pursuit of eternal verities. . . .[18]

In this passage, at least, Peirce locates himself squarely in the cognitivists' camp.

Pragmatism

The term 'pragmatism' has been used in a variety of senses. It is most closely associated, however, with the views of William James and John Dewey, and for them there seems to be one sense which is central. For James and Dewey pragmatism makes the claim that Peirce's separation of science from practice is false and that there is instead a fundamental analogy between the justification of acceptance in the context of scientific inquiry and its justification in the context of practical deliberation. For both, justification must in part be given relative to the actions for which the accepted proposition serves as a basis and to purposes these actions fulfill. Purely epistemic criteria are not in themselves sufficient to make an evaluation; the "dross of subjectivity," as Peirce calls it, infects all inquiry, both practical and theoretical. In its earliest form this was stated as the view that "the true is the useful": a true proposition is one that proves useful as a basis for action. As such it has been the subject of extensive criticisms dating back to the beginning of this century. As a theory of justified acceptance rather than truth it has been restated by recent writers, but this revision, as I shall argue in Chapter 5, has flaws as fundamental as the original. A more restricted form of pragmatism can be defended, however, by reformulating criteria for rational acceptance in terms of comparisons between the potential costs of the accepted proposition being mistaken and the costs of acquiring evidence.

Pragmatism can concede that the justification of acceptance is made relative to procedural rules to which inquiry must conform. But these rules are regarded by it as themselves derived in part from the operation of human interests and purposes. This view has been articulated by Jurgen Habermas. The rules of both the natural and social (or cultural) sciences, Habermas says,

arise from actual structures of human life: from structures of a species that reproduces its life both through learning processes of socially organized labor and processes of mutual understanding in interactions mediated in ordinary language. These basic conditions of life have an interest structure.

The meaning of the validity of statements derivable within...inquiry in the natural and cultural sciences is determined in relation to this structure.[19]

We shall return to the problem of determining exactly how procedural rules are related to interests in Chapter 4.

It is important to distinguish the central issues between cognitivism and pragmatism from two irrelevant issues with which they have often been confused. That our purposes play an important role in determining which questions to ask is not in dispute. Advocates of cognitivism can concede that the benefit we expect to reap from their answers will determine that some questions are selected for investigation, while others are ignored. Obviously, the causes of cancer are selected for study while those of benign growths ignored because of society's greater stake in finding the former over the latter. The history of science is replete with examples of an inquiry being undertaken as a means to solving a practical problem, as astronomy was pursued in ancient and medieval times for its anticipated help in solving problems of crop planning and navigation. At issue is only whether or not, after a question has been posed, the acceptance of a specific hypothesis as answer to it is to be justified by purely epistemic criteria, or whether purposes also have a role in this decision.

A second feature of inquiry is also not at issue. It is that individual investigators often bring to their fields of study biases, prejudices, and personal needs that influence the results of their research. The fact that an investigator wants a particular result often leads to certain relevant data being ignored. Sometimes the desire for quick publication and immediate economic gain will motivate him or her to cut short a survey of available evidence. In such cases it seems obvious that we would brand such actions as irrational and open to criticism. The fact that such behavior *does* occur is agreed by all to have no bearing on deciding whether or not it *should* occur.[20] As for the first, discussions of the relation between "facts" and "values" have sometimes been marred by the introduction of this extraneous issue.

Before turning to our systematic discussions of the alternative theories just outlined, we need to explain more carefully the nature of acceptance in relation to belief and certainty, the psychological states which have been the focus of most discussions in epistemology. This is the task in the first three sections of the next chapter.

Chapter 2

Knowledge and Rational Belief

The pragmatic theory outlined in the previous section has been the object of strenuous and consistent attack in this century. Why has this occurred? One reason seems to be that the problem of stating criteria for rational acceptance has usually been formulated as that of evaluating a belief as rational. Rational belief has been, in turn, discussed in the context of modern epistemology as one of the conditions for knowledge as a state a person is in when he stands in an appropriate relation to the world about him. In this chapter I review some comparisons and contrasts between epistemology's central concepts of knowledge, certainty, and belief on the the one hand and acceptance on the other. In Section 2.1 the classical conception of knowledge as true justified belief is outlined, along with the problem posed by Gettier-type examples. Here it is shown how features of our use of 'know' in everyday communication situations are inconsistent with the necessary and sufficient conditions for knowledge that epistemology has attempted to provide. The second section introduces justified certainty as a condition for knowledge, and discusses skepticism as a consequence that has been drawn by some philosophers from this condition. The denial here of any contrast between what is called "absolute certainty" and "practical certainty" is crucial for the case for the pragmatic theory of rational acceptance developed in Chapter 4. In Section 2.3 belief is distinguished from acceptance. Of particular interest to us is the fact that belief may be involuntary, while acceptance is invariably a voluntary decision. This feature is used in the final section to contrast reliabilism as a theory of rational belief invoking a causal condition to the alternative theories of rational acceptance considered in later chapters. No causal condition can be applied to acceptance as a voluntary decision implying a commitment to action.

2.1 USES OF 'KNOW'

The problem of distinguishing knowledge from true belief or opinion is stated by Plato in the *Theaetetus*. To know, Plato says, is not only to have a belief that is true. The judges of a trial can be persuaded by the eloquent oratory of a lawyer to believe that a person is guilty of a crime, and the person may, in fact, be guilty. But such a belief does not constitute knowledge. The belief must be "combined with reason," that is, arrived at in such a way as to ensure its truth. Only if the belief is in this way justified or rational, rather than one which just happens to be true, can it be said to constitute knowledge.[1]

Implicit in this epistemological tradition is what is sometimes referred to as the "spectator view of knowledge," the view that to know is to be in an appropriate relation to an independent world and that we as spectators of this world must arrive at our beliefs by methods that insure that this appropriate relation obtains. Whether it obtains is independent of any subjective purposes or emotions that the spectator may have, and hence a rational belief must be dispassionate and exclude any irrelevant interests. It is within this tradition that Keith Lehrer states the requirement for what he calls "completely justified belief."

> A man may believe things because of the comfort it gives him, because of greed, because of hate, and so forth. Such beliefs may be totally irrelevant to the question of what the man is completely justified in believing. It is only those beliefs which he would retain in an impartial and disinterested search for truth that sustain justification aimed at veracity.[2]

In order to evaluate this view we must first examine the framework in which the problem for stating criteria for rational belief is usually discussed. This is one in which the avowed goal is to state necessary and sufficient conditions for a person X knowing a proposition p. Usually these conditions are (i) that the proposition p be true; (ii) that X believe that p; and (iii) that X be justified in believing that p, or that X's belief be rational. In some versions conditions (ii) and (iii) are formulated as requiring that X not only simply believe p but be certain of it and be justified in this certainty. These strengthened certainty requirements and the difficulties they present will be discussed in the next section.

Discussions in recent years have focused on the problem of accounting within the classical framework for examples that seem to satisfy the three conditions just listed, but fail to constitute knowledge. The following example, similar to one first proposed by Edmund Gettier, illustrates the difficulty with the classical conditions.[3] Suppose that in a person X's office there is a Mr. Nogot who has given X evidence to support the proposition that he owns a Ford, e.g. has referred to his car as a Ford, pointed to a Ford in the street and claimed it was his. Then if Nogot has been reliable in the past, we would regard X as being justified in his belief that Nogot has a Ford. From the proposition expressed by 'Nogot owns a Ford' we can logically deduce 'Someone in X's office owns a Ford'. It seems evident that if a proposition p logically entails another proposition *q,* then if *X* is justified in believing that *p* he is also justified in believing in *q.* Hence, *X* is justified in believing that someone in his office owns a Ford. Let us suppose that in *X*'s office there is another worker, a Mr. Havit who does own a Ford, but that *X* is unaware of this. We will also suppose that Nogot was shamming, that he really didn't own a Ford, but had mislead X into believing that he did. Then we can say that the proposition that someone owns a Ford is true, that *X* believes it, and is justified in holding this belief on the evidence provided by him. But we can certainly conclude that he doesn't know this proposition to be true, contrary to the classical definition of knowledge as justified true belief.

In response to these Gettier-type examples philosophers have attempted to devise a fourth condition which when added to the original three will provide adequate conditions for knowledge.[4] All are designed to rule out the element of accident or luck, e.g. *X*'s luck that Havit happens to own a Ford, occurring when justified true belief falls short of knowledge. Given the general assumption of traditional epistemology that to know is to be in an appropriate relation to some independent state of affairs *S*, it was natural to seek some relation between a given *S* and the subject *X* which insures knowledge. The most influential solution seems virtually dictated by the assumptions behind the search. It claims the relation to be a causal relation between the state *S* and *X*'s belief; only if the state *S* described by the true proposition *p* causes *X*'s belief in *p* can *X* be said to know *p.*[5] As we shall see in the final section of this chapter, such a causal relation is also invoked in attempts to specify conditions for rational belief.

The results of all these attempts, however, have been disappointing. For each proposed solution new counterexamples have been adduced showing its inadequacy. This has required increasingly complicated conditions to be added whose only virtue, it seems, is their ability to account for the counterexamples to previous attempts. Furthermore, not even the necessity of the classical conditions has been conceded in recent discussions, with some questioning whether *X*'s knowing *p* requires X's believing it.[6]

The inconclusiveness of these alternative lists of conditions is symptomatic of a fundamental difficulty in the classical epistemological program. Invariably analyses are directed towards the third person use of the verb 'know', with examples given that describe, on the basis of perfect information available to the epistemologist, the relevant states of affairs, the belief state of a person, and the evidence upon which the belief is based. In actual communication situations, however, we say of others that they "know" things in a variety of different ways and in these situations information is limited. Moreover, there is a first person use of 'know' that exhibits features very different from those of the third person uses. Given this variety of uses, it is to be expected that any given list of necessary and sufficient conditions will be defective.

To see this let us first consider the first person use of 'know'. As J. L. Austin pointed out, it is one in which a person gives his guarantee or strong endorsement of the proposition being asserted.[7] For X to say 'I know Jones will come' is for X to express his conviction that Jones will arrive, to give his personal guarantee of the arrival and stake his reputation for veracity on it. Here to use 'know' is to assert the truth of the proposition, and in this sense knowledge requires truth. But it seems to exclude 'believe', since this term is used to express hesitancy of the kind ruled out by the strong endorsement. Moreover, since it functions to indicate that the proposition is to be taken as a guarantee, 'know' does not describe the psychological state of the speaker nor some special relation between the speaker and environmental states of affairs.

When we turn to third person uses of 'know' we find very different conditions holding. In standard communication situations we ask about knowledge for two main reasons. The first is to find out whether a person X is a potential source of information about a state of affairs. Almost invariably this question is more general than the desired information. For example, we ask 'Does X know the time of day?' or 'Does X know the location (color, size, etc.) of object Z?' prior to receiving from X the specific information sought after in the form of an asserted proposition. Philosophers have also noted a nonpropositional "acquaintance" sense of 'know' in which we say 'X knows George' or 'X knows the taste of such and such wine'.[8] To ask 'Does X know George?' is often preliminary to asking of X further information about the individual or item with which he is acquainted, e.g. 'Is George tall?', 'Is the wine sweet?', etc. In all these uses of 'know' it is implied that the person X bears a special relationship to some state of affairs or other or has access to evidence unavailable to the person posing the question, e.g. has seen a clock, has observed the location of Z, or has met George. But so far as X is such a potential source of information his state of belief and hence the rationality of this belief does not seem to be in question, and can be regarded as irrelevant. The expert chicken sexer can instinctively discriminate male from female chicks without first forming proposition-directed beliefs based on evidence. If he is invariably or almost invariably correct with his discriminations, he can be said to "know" in the sense of being a reliable source of information, but it is not necessary that he have rational beliefs.

The second reason that may exist for asking about a person X's state of knowledge is to determine X's capacity as a potential recipient of information or addressee of a command. We often inquire about another's acquaintance form of knowledge in order to determine whether he or she will understand some later statement or command we are planning to make. Thus, we ask '*X*, do you know George?' prior to conveying information through sentences such as 'George is on vacation' or 'Call George on the telephone'. If *X* lacked the prior acquaintance, he would not be able to identify the intended referent of the utterances. Sometimes it is not a prior acquaintance but only descriptive information that is asked about, again for the purpose of determining whether identification is possible. Thus, we ask '*X*, do you know who (which, what) *Y* is (are)?' to determine whether *X* could identify the individual or class of indivi- duals *Y* if the term '*Y*' were to be used as the subject of a sentence. Sometimes determining knowledge is also important as a means of preventing redundancy of information, as when we ask 'Does *X* know that *p*?' in order to avoid unnecessarily repeating to *X* what would be of no value to him.

In none of these recipient-directed senses of 'know' can we find all the conditions for knowledge listed by epistemologists. In the nonproposi- tional acquaintance sense where capacity for identification is in question belief and truth are irrelevant, though a relation to what is known is presupposed. Where the ability to identify on the basis of a description is being asked for, belief is relevant. But no relation is presupposed, and the truth of these beliefs is not essential. Someone could mistakenly believe that George was the man who immigrated recently from Russia. If it was not Russia but Hungary from which George came, that person might still correctly identify the man being referred to, and in this sense know who he is. Where determination of nonredundancy is being asked by 'Does *X* know that *p*?', the truth of p is, of course, presupposed, and it may be presupposed that *X* is in a certain relation to the state of affairs being described. But belief, and hence rational belief, need not be assumed. Asking of the expert chicken sexer whether he knows that this chick is a male is not to ask whether he believes this or whether he has good evidence for the belief. For him information about the chick would be redundant, but not because of his being in a state of belief.

The artificial, contrived sense of 'know' as stated in the definitions of epistemologists in the classical tradition, then, seems only loosely related to 'know' as used to answer questions about the sources and recipients of information. Moreover, some attempts at specifying conditions for knowledge would seem to make it impossible for us to ever ascribe 'knows that *p*' of another. In an attempt to account for Gettier-type examples Lehrer and Paxson have proposed the additional condition that for *X* to know that *p* there must not be some other true proposition *q* which in conjunction with the existing evidence would make it unreason- able for *X* to believe that *p*.[9] This can be applied to the case of *X* knowing that someone owns a Ford on the basis of the false but justified belief that Nogot owns one, since *X*'s realizing Nogot doesn't own a Ford would undermine his belief. But we as participants in actual communication situations are never in a position to assert that such a possible defeator is absent when attempting to assess potential information sources or recipients of information. Hence, we could never make assertions of the form '*X* knows that *p*' in the way we actually do. I think it could be shown that similar considerations would hold for the other intricate candidates that have been proposed in recent epistemology for the fourth additional condition. The philosopher can describe his own hypothetical examples from a position of omniscience, and from his God-like perspective determine whether his conditions are satisfied. However, we could never be in a position to actually determine this in the situations of partial information typical when we make our everyday assessments of knowledge.

In summary, the attempt to state necessary and sufficient conditions for 'know' in its propositional sense cannot possibly be successful given the variety of uses of the verb to guarantee in the first person and assess information sources and recipients in the third person. Moreover, we are not capable of determining whether or not the conditions proposed have in fact been satisfied, and hence could never make assertions about knowledge of the kind we actually do make. Recent epistemology offers, therefore, little promise as a means of explicating the term 'know' as actually used. Yet it is within its framework that the problem of stating criteria for rational or justified belief has been undertaken.

2.2   THE CERTAINTY REQUIREMENT

Following the Platonic model, Ayer has stated three necessary and sufficient conditions for propositional knowledge. They are "first that what one is said to know be true, secondly that one be sure of it, and thirdly that one should have the right to be sure."[10] This substitution of "sureness" or certainty for mere belief that results in a definition of knowledge as justified true certainty has been common in the history of philosophy. The intuition behind it seems to be as follows. Certainty, like knowledge, is an all-or-nothing state that a person is in. We cannot be more or less certain that it rained last night, any more than we can more or less know that it rained. A belief in a proposition *p*, on the other hand, admits of degrees, with certainty that *p* at one limiting extreme and certainty that *p* is not the case, or complete doubt, at the other. Those making the substitution hold that any degree of belief less than certainty will not support a knowledge claim. Many biologists believe, for example, that about 60 million years ago there was a cataclysmic event that profoundly altered the evolution of life on this planet, and the belief is supported by some evidence. But they cannot be said to know that this event took place, since they are still not certain of it. In contrast, I am certain that it rained last night: the streets are wet; I heard a characteristic sound on the roof; etc. Because of this certainty and its justification I can be said to know of the rain.

Once the belief condition has been strengthened to a certainty condition, however, problems immediately arise. The most fundamental of them is that of skepticism, the problem whether a person can ever be said to know any proposition. Knowledge is impossible, argues the skeptic, because certainty as a psychological state is not in itself sufficient. People can feel conviction about many things and later realize that they were deluded and hence really did not know, as those in the Middle Ages who were convinced that the earth was flat, and the many in colonial times who believed that there were witches. As Ayer states in his third condition, we must "have the right to be sure"; our certainty must be justified. But certainty could only be justified, it is claimed, if there were no possibility of being mistaken, and this possibility is always present, even for what we take to be most obvious. I see in front of me a piece of white paper on my desk. In such a situation I would feel justified in saying 'I am certain there is a piece of white paper in front of me'. But there is at least the possibility that the lighting in my room may be abnormal, making what is red look white, that mirrors have been cleverly constructed to make it seem as though the paper were there, etc. In this sense I can never claim certainty for even the most obvious propositions reporting matters of fact. Many versions of skepticism do single out as immune from error a special class of propositions, those describing direct experiences, and hence concede them to be certain. Thus, it is thought that I can at least assert with certainty 'I have a visual image of whiteness and a certain shape'. But in the absence of any deductive inferences from such experiential reports to 'There is a white piece of paper in front me' this kind of certainty, even if it were possible to attain, would fail to be transmitted to descriptions of the objects in our environment.

It is always possible, of course, to take precautions against possible error, and these precautions might be thought of as warranting certainty. Thus, I could check on the lighting, carefully look to see if mirrors are around, check my responses to see if I am suffering from delusions, etc., before describing the piece of paper. To this skepticism has two replies. The first is to note that for every precaution taken there is still some other possibility of error that remains, e.g. that after checking for lighting and mirrors there still remains the possibility of an indefinite number of physiological abnormalities in me that might produce error. The second reply is to utilize a strategy, followed by Descartes in his *Meditations,* of conceiving of the possibility of powerful forces that distort in ways that could not possibly be detected. Peter Unger follows this strategy in his defense of skepticism by conceiving of a malevolent scientist with extraordinary powers who implants electrodes in the brains of subjects and causes them to have the experiences that typically accompany seeing objects like pieces of paper, though none of these objects are in fact present. Since any experience could be in principle induced by such a scientist, and there would be no way for us to detect what is being done to us, Unger argues that no experience could ever be taken as conclusive evidence that no such distortions are being produced, no matter how great the precautions we take against error.[11]

The skeptic can concede that we do in fact use the word 'certain' in everyday situations, and we believe ourselves justified in saying we are certain that it rained last night, that there is paper on the desk, that the earth is roughly spherical, etc. In all such cases, they claim, we are using the word in the sense of "practical" or "subjective" certainty, as contrasted with the "absolute," "theoretical," or "philosophical" certainty that is required for knowledge.[12] Practical certainty in a proposition *p* is context-dependent and implies a willingness to use *p* as a basis for action. Often we are willing to ascribe adjectives in one context but withhold them in others, as we may assert of a lawn that it is "flat" for the purposes of hosting a barbecue party on it, but assert it is "not flat" for the purposes of playing croquet. Because the actions relevant to the applications of the term differ, our ascriptions differ. In the same way, we can say we are "certain" of a given proposition in one context, but be "uncertain" of it in another. I may say I am certain that a given rope will bear 200 pounds if it is to be used to lift a rock, but say I am uncertain of its bearing this weight if it is to be used on a rock-climbing expedition where lives at stake. The risk of a mistake leads us to refuse to apply the term in this latter context, whereas in the relatively risk-free context of rock lifting it was applied. It is this practical sense of 'certain', the skeptic argues, that we use in everyday life, a use that can be justified relative to the special circumstances in which it is applied.

It is in the very different absolute sense of 'certain' that the skeptic wants to maintain we are never justified in claiming certainty for any empirical proposition. Absolute certainty is justified only when all possibility of error has been eliminated. This is a limit that we can approach, as we take more and more precautions against error. But since error is always possible, it is a limit that can never be reached. The analogy to the use of the adjective 'flat' is again helpful. An absolutely flat surface can be defined as a surface free from any depressions or protuberances. As such it can be successively approached by lawns, golf greens, wood table tops, and polished marble surfaces, but can never be actually reached. Every surface will have at least microscopic irregularities. In this absolute sense 'This is flat' will be false when used to describe any given surface. In the same way 'I am certain that p' can never be justified, no matter what empirical proposition p is under consideration, if 'certain' is taken in its absolute sense.[13]

In the absolute sense of 'certain' just employed we must concede the skeptics' conclusion: every empirical proposition is liable to error and to being corrected on some later occasion. But we must immediately recognize also that the term 'absolutely certain' is a philosopher's invention, a technical term with an arbitrarily stipulated meaning that has little relevance to the term as ordinarily used. As Wittgenstein first pointed out, in introducing their term philosophers in the skeptical tradition have at the same time coined a new term and traded on the meaning of the existing term in claiming their conclusion as a correction of common sense. When I say 'I am certain there is a white piece of paper before me' I am not corrected by the skeptics' claim 'We can never be certain about any empirical proposition', for his absolute sense of 'certain' is very different from mine. Moreover, the skeptics' term destroys the contrast between 'certain' and 'uncertain' that gives each term its meaning. In the ordinary sense of practical certainty to say 'I am certain that *p*' means 'I am not uncertain that *p*', that no practical doubt in *p* is justifiable relative to the context in which it is being asserted. But since 'absolutely certain' can never be applied to any proposition, since its use has been prohibited by definition, no such contrast is available for the skeptics' sense of 'certain'. What skeptics leave us with, then, is an arbitrarily defined sense of 'certain' that guarantees that we will never be able to make the contrasts essential to any effective use of the term.[14]

So far we have been discussing the problem of skepticism in relation to perceptual propositions describing objects of our immediate environment. In the next chapter we will turn to the application of skeptical arguments that follow Hume in being directed towards our knowledge of generalizations inductively supported by propositions describing particular objects or events. Here the skeptical conclusion merely restates the obvious fact that no empirical hypothesis can be deductively inferred from supporting evidence, and hence, even if we could be certain of this evidence, this certainty cannot be transmitted to the hypothesis under consideration. There remains always the possibility of error and later correction. This conclusion can also be reformulated as stating that we cannot justifiably assert a hypothesis as true relative to evidence; we can at best assert it to be "probably" true or determine its "degree of confirmation." When skeptics conclude in this manner that we can never be justifiably certain of any empirical generalization they are again using 'certain' in a very special, eccentric sense. The rest of us contrast our certainty that the sun will rise tomorrow, that lead sinks in water, or that a virus causes pneumonia with our uncertainty as to whether vitamin C is a cure for the common cold or the universe will continue to indefinitely expand. Similarly, in the context of scientific inquiry 'certain' is used to indicate the transition of a proposition to inclusion in background knowledge of the kind discussed in Section 1.3, while 'uncertain' indicates what is given only provisional acceptance.

The certainty requirement, we may recall, is stated in the context of defining a knowledge relation holding between a knower and some independent state of affairs. Given the assumptions of the classical framework in which such a definition is sought, it follows that mere "practical" certainty cannot be regarded as fulfilling this requirement. The knowledge relation is, after all, thought to be an "objective" one that can be described as either holding or failing to hold relative to examples carefully constructed by epistemologists detailing all relevant information. Practical certainty requires the introduction of "subjective" factors and can vary with the particular context of purposes and anticipated actions in which the agent finds himself. It must then be rejected, it is argued, as a condition in favor of a justified absolute certainty requirement that does guarantee knowledge. But since this kind of requirement can never be fulfilled, knowledge becomes impossible. In this way the basic assumptions of classical epistemology have insured that its central problem, since Hume, has remained that of skepticism.

We have seen how in the first person 'know' is typically used to offer one's guarantee of the truth of a proposition being asserted. Used in the first person 'certain' seems to perform a similar function. To say 'I am certain that it will rain' is not, as many philosophers have noted, to describe one's psychological state. For if it were a psychological description, on what would it be based? Surely not on any accompanying feeling, for I can claim certainty without being aware of any such feeling.[15] Nor is the sentence describing a dispositional state of myself, for I rarely observe my own behavior over a period of time prior to producing an utterance of it. Instead, the prefix 'I am certain that . . .', like 'I know that . . .', serves to convey the illocutionary force of the proposition expressed by the sentence radical 'it is raining' that follows. We can sometimes convey conviction by the tone of voice with which we utter our assertions. But this is sometimes misunderstood and not available if writing is our means of communication, and hence 'certain' is used to make explicit the force of an utterance and convey a contrast to the hesitancy conveyed by other prefixes such as 'I believe that . . .' or 'I think that . . .'. 'I am certain that p', unlike these other psychological prefixes, indicates the speaker's unqualified terminal acceptance of p.

Used in the third person to say 'He (she) is certain that p', however, 'certain' is used to describe the psychological state of the person being referred to. What then is the relationship between this use of the word and the acceptance of a proposition? To answer this requires examining the relationships between belief in general and acceptance, and to this we now turn.

2.3 BELIEF AND ACCEPTANCE

The acceptance or rejection of a proposition as true or false is a dateable psychological act, and the same proposition accepted by a person at a given time may be later rejected by him. These psychological acts are conceptually related to the public speech acts of assent, dissent, assertion, and denial as their necessary conditions. X asks Y, 'Is it raining outside?', and Y answers 'Yes', thereby assenting to the proposition that it is raining outside. Y could not be said to sincerely assent to this proposition if he had not accepted it as true. A similar relationship holds between his dissent 'No' and the rejection of the proposition. This relationship holds if X were to assert to Y 'It is raining' or deny the proposition with 'It is not raining'. Though he may have uttered the words, X would not have performed the speech acts of assertion or denial if he himself had not accepted or rejected the proposition being expressed. Acceptance (and also rejection) need not be publicly expressed by assent or assertion (dissent or denial). But if all unexpressed thought is some kind of interpretation of "inner speech," as many psychologists and philosophers have speculated, then it is plausible to regard acceptance that is unexpressed as an internal assent to or assertion of mental analogues of sentences.

When we ascribe belief or certainty to another person, we are ascribing to him or her a dispositional state that persists over an indefinite period of time.[16] All dispositional states are ascribed on the basis of past behavior and are used to predict future behavior. We can ascribe elasticity to a particular rubber band Z, for example, on the basis of observing how rubber bands similar to it have stretched when forces have been exerted on them. On the basis of the ascription we can go on to claim that if a force were exerted on Z it would also stretch. For beliefs as dispositional states what are the behavioral bases and predictions? They can be of the nonverbal sort described by Ryle in *The Concept of Mind*,[17] as when we say of a person that he believes a pond's ice is thin on the basis of his skating warily on the edge of the pond and predict that if he heard a crack he would rush for safety. But often we ascribe beliefs to others on the basis of what they say and predict from these ascriptions what they would be willing to assert or assent to. On the basis of a person X asserting 'It will rain' or assenting with apparent sincerity to this sentence we can conclude that he believes it will rain. More generally, we assume in our belief ascriptions what Kripke calls the "Disquotational Principle:" If a person speaking English assents to a sentence 'p', then he believes that p, where the indirect speech form reporting the content of X's belief replaces the sentence 'p' to which X assents.[18] If X speaks some language other than English, then the description of his belief state must be formulated in the English sentence we would use to translate his foreign language sentence. Thus, from a German's assenting to '*Es regnet*' we can conclude 'This German believes that it is raining', for 'It is raining' would be used by us to express that to which he is assenting. In this way we ascribe beliefs on the basis of verbal behavior.

It is possible to challenge the Disquotational Principle. Robert Stalnaker, for example, contends on pragmatic grounds that it could be reasonable for a person X to accept a proposition *p* as true without X believing *p* to be true. This can occur, he claims, "when it is known that the difference between what is accepted and the truth will have no significant effect on the answer to the particular question being asked."[19] Thus, X could accept 'This table is 4 feet long', while believing on the basis of other information that the table's length is more exactly 3 feet and 11⅜ inches. That acceptance is relative to the specific information content conveyed by a sentence and that this can vary with context is an important insight that we shall return to at the end of Chapter 4. But it is mistaken to appeal to it as a way of distinguishing acceptance from belief. What X accepts is that the table is 4 feet long *as an approximation,* as within a permissible interval of error, and what he believes is perfectly consistent with this. There is thus no acceptance not accompanied by belief.

In contrast, what Kripke calls the "Converse Disquotational Principle" allowing us to predict verbal behavior from beliefs does encounter genuine difficulties. Suppose X to be a speaker of English who believes that *p*. Can we then conclude that X will assent to the sentence '*p*', assuming there are adequate inducements to respond, that he is sincere, etc.? Here I think we should answer in the negative. Beliefs, especially those inculcated in early childhood, can be held without our realizing that we hold them, and it seems quite possible to believe without acknowledging it. Thus, someone could show us by his fearful behavior that he believes in ghosts but quite sincerely deny it when asked. On the other hand, if X were to accept the proposition that *p*, it does follow that he would assent to the sentence '*p*', since we cannot accept and be unaware. It seems to be a confusion between acceptance and belief, then, that leads to our applying the converse disquotational principle to the latter.

This confusion is common in philosophical literature, and has had unfortunate consequences in discussions of rational belief, as we shall see in the next section. Three important differences have already been noted. First, belief is a dispositional state of indefinite duration, while acceptance is a dateable psychological act. Secondly, belief admits of degrees ranging from certainty in a proposition *p* to certainty of *p*'s negation, while acceptance (like knowledge and certainty) is all-or-nothing. A person either accepts p or he doesn't, though we can, as noted in Section 1.3, distinguish between terminal and provisional acceptance. The third difference was discussed in Section 1.2, where we contrasted the commitment to action required by acceptance of fact-stating propositions in the context of practical inferences to the weaker conclusion that an action is rational following from premises expressing beliefs.

Besides these differences there is also that between an act and its result. To accept as true the proposition that it is raining results in one's believing that it is raining, much as the result of shutting the door is that the door is shut. As we saw in Section 1.3, background knowledge consists of beliefs that result from prior acts of terminal acceptance. In such cases an act logically entails a state as its result. But a state of affairs does not in the same way entail an act. A door can be shut, though no one shuts it; it may just happen to be shut, perhaps by a gust of wind. In an analogous way a person can believe that *p* without ever necessarily having accepted *p* if the belief were acquired without his being aware of its acquisition, as for beliefs inculcated in early childhood. He simply happens to be in the state of belief.

This assymmetry between acceptance and belief stems from what is surely their most fundamental difference. Our acceptance of a proposition *p* is invariably voluntary and within our control. We must decide to either (terminally) accept *p* or refuse to accept it. To refuse to accept *p* is to either provisionally accept it, that is, accept *p* as a candidate for testing, reject *p*, that is, accept its negation not-*p*, or remain undecided about *p* and undertake no commitments to subsequent actions. Acceptance and each of these alternatives as acts within the control of the agent are open to evaluation by such terms as 'ought', 'rational', or 'justified'. If one of these acts ought not to have been performed, we evaluate them by 'irrational' or 'unjustified'.

In contrast to acts of acceptance and rejection, belief and disbelief in a proposition seem to be psychological states over which we have no control. Like most others, I happen to believe that the earth is roughly spherical, that the duration of individual human life has an upper limit of about one hundered and twenty years, and that man has evolved from lower animals. None of these are beliefs that I can be said to now choose to have, and it would be impossible for me to now adopt the attitude of disbelief towards them. In this sense states of belief are involuntary. But if they are involuntary, then it would seem impossible to say that a person ought to hold a given belief, and hence say that the belief is rational or justified, for 'ought' and its attendant normative terms have no application to the involuntary. I cannot be said to be under an obligation to live less than one hundred and twenty years, sleep periodically, or inhale oxygen by breathing. As beyond our control, these activities, like belief states, are regarded as incapable of evaluation.[20] What applies to beliefs generally also applies to certainty as a special limiting kind of belief. Our certainty in a proposition is no more within our control than is a tentative belief and, therefore, is also not subject to evaluation.

We do, of course, apply the normative terms 'rational' and 'justified' to the beliefs of others, saying, for example, that it is irrational for X to believe in ghosts or that his belief in the creationist theory of evolution is unjustified. In making such evaluation we are, I think, doing one of three things. First, we may be criticizing the proposition that X believes as one we regard as being what we as evaluators should not accept given the available evidence. In this case we are not criticizing X as a person, but simply refusing to endorse what he believes. Secondly, if X's belief is the result of his accepting at some earlier time the proposition he now believes, then we may be criticizing this earlier acceptance. X may have come to believe in the creationist theory on the basis of an evangelical preacher widely regarded as a charlatan. We could then criticize X's belief by criticizing his acceptance of the theory on the basis of such an unreliable source. And finally, though a belief in a proposition *p* may itself be beyond our control, whether we persist in it can often be determined by whether we reject *p* on some later occasion on the basis of further evidence. Thus, we may criticize X's beliefs in either ghosts or creationism if he deliberately ignores evidence, which if considered, would lead to his rejecting what he now believes. In all three cases, then, it is some relevant act of acceptance that is being evaluated as irrational or unjustified. The belief is open to criticism only so far as it is the result of such an act.

So far we have been considering the acceptance/belief distinction relative only to examples of propositions based on other propositions as evidence. When we turn to perceptual propositions it becomes more difficult to make the distinction in the manner that we have. I see the white paper in front of me and accept the proposition expressed by 'This paper is white' as true. As a result I come to believe the paper to be white. But it seems difficult in such cases to claim a contrast between the belief as beyond my control and the proposition's acceptance as voluntary. On seeing the paper I seem to have as little choice in accepting the proposition as in holding the belief. The sight of the paper seems to compel acceptance, and hence no voluntary/involuntary distinction parallels that between acceptance and belief.

But no exception need be made for perception if we contrast the situations in which we normally form perceptual beliefs from special situations in which the costs of our being mistaken are much higher. In normal situations we accept on the basis of direct perception without any further efforts being taken, and acceptance seems to follow automatically. But there can be situations of risk or importance where acceptance would be delayed pending further checks. For a physician the color of complexion may be an important symptom in diagnosing an ailment. A patient's face may look red, but if the physician is an unusual environment he or she may choose to check lighting conditions before deciding that the face is in fact red and prescribing a cure. Similarly, a pointer on a scientific instrument may seem to be aligned with a certain number on the instrument's scale. If the measurement being made is routine, then what is apparently the reading may be accepted as being the actual reading. But if the reading is of importance, perhaps crucial to the completion of a long and expensive program of research, then extra precautions would probably be taken to ensure that the angle at which the instrument is read insures an accurate measurement. There are innumerable other examples of this kind. As we saw in Section 2.2, skeptics have emphasized how the possibility of error is present even in direct perception. Normally we discount this possibility, and if an object *S* seems on the basis of direct observation to have property *P* we accept '*S* is *P*' as being true. But even here the acceptance is voluntary and is, in effect, a decision not to take the precautions that could be taken if more were at stake. Those occasions where we do check before accepting should make us realize that on all occasions this option is before us, a kind of ace up our sleeve that need not be played.

The features of the belief/acceptance distinction just discussed are important to us as a preliminary to our now considering an influential theory of rational belief that has been formulated in recent years.

2.4. RELIABILISM

The theory known as *reliabilism* employs what is referred to as the "thermometer model" of justified or rational belief.[21] Just as a thermometer registers the temperature of the immediate environment, so a belief state is claimed to register an environmental state of affairs. We can conclude that a given temperature reading of a thermometer is reliable if it regularly registers the temperature of the locale accurately. In an analogous way a belief of a person can be said to be justified if it is the causal effect of an environmental state of affairs *S* and *S* produces this belief effect by a reliable process, a process that regularly, though not necessarily invariably, produces true beliefs that correspond to *S*. As themselves the result of a long evolutionary history in which natural selection has tended to eliminate those that produce beliefs failing to match environmental conditions, most belief-inducing processes are reliable. But a particular belief may be produced by one that is not, and in this case it must be evaluated as unjustified or irrational.

The reliabilist theory can be regarded as part of the general project of giving a naturalistic account of belief using the causal terminology of the empirical sciences. Following Davidson many philosophers have regarded beliefs as at least part of the reasons for a person's actions and also the causes of these actions. Why did the man carry the umbrella? One explanation may be that he did it because he wanted to stay dry and believed that carrying the umbrella was the best way to realize his end. In this explanation we cite the belief in conjunction with the desire as the cause of the action. Reliabilism, on the other hand, views beliefs as causal effects and attempts to explicate their rationality in terms of the nature of external processes by which the beliefs are produced. Such an externalist theory is to be contrasted with the internalist theories considered in the next chapter, which state criteria for rationality in terms of logical relations between propositions. If the belief is a perceptual belief, for example, my belief that the paper before me is white, then these processes include the physiological processes of retinal stimulation and the encoding and decoding of information transmitted to the brain. If the belief is nonperceptual but based on perceptual evidence, e.g. my belief that all robins eggs are blue, then the processes will be those in which some beliefs cause others.[22] Irrelevant to the reliability of these processes are logical relations between evidence and the proposition it supports. For both perceptual and nonperceptual beliefs, the desires or purposes of the person are also regarded as irrelevant to the justification of belief; what is alone relevant is whether these processes tend to produce beliefs matching environmental states of affairs, and whether this tendency can be determined independently of any "subjective" considerations.

Fatal defects of the theory become evident when we look closely at the procedures that it must claim we use in actually making our assessments of rationality. These procedures can be most clearly applied to perceptual beliefs. Consider a situation in which we are attempting to assess the reliability of a subject X's mechanisms of visual perception in conditions of poor illumination by comparing his perceptual beliefs with the states of affairs they are about. Thus, we show to X differently colored objects in a dimly lit room and ask him questions such as 'Is this object red?', 'Is that object blue?', etc. From his assents or dissents to the questions we infer by the Disquotational Principle of the previous section that X does or does not believe that this object is red or that object is blue. Then we compare his beliefs with what we accept as true, that is, compare them with what we call the relevant "facts" in order to determine whether they are true or false. Let us suppose that after many such tests we find that three-fourths of the time when X believes that an object is red his belief is true, while on the remaining occasions his beliefs about redness are false. There is thus a probability of .75 that X is correct. On some specific occasion when X assents to 'This is red' in the same lighting conditions we should then be able to determine, according to the reliabilist theory, whether X's belief is rational.

But can we? There is first the problem of determining the types of states of affairs and processes to which X's beliefs are relevant.[23] Let us suppose that X is discriminating red only from blue in the above experiments. There would still be an indefinite variety of other colors that would be relevant to his color discriminations. He may be able to distinguish yellow from red with a .7 probability of success, orange from red with a .65 probability, or orangish-red from red with .60 probability. Which probability should be used in assessing the reliability of X's current belief? Goldman requires that the types that can be discriminated be "maximally specific" or the "narrowest type" producing the belief in question.[24] But if the subject is faced only with the problem of distinguishing red from blue, it seems unreasonable to apply to him the probability of success for distinguishing the more closely related orangish-red from red. The degree of specificity is much higher than than warranted by the problem at hand.

Closely related to this problem of discriminations is that of determining the truth of what X assents to. Let us suppose that we are asking X about the shapes of objects, and X consistently assents to 'This is square' when presented with objects whose angles diverge from ninety degrees and whose sides are slightly unequal. Has he said what is true? Without standards of exactness it seems impossible to say. Sufficiently precise measurements would show all our normal everyday objects to have slightly divergent angles and side lengths. Yet for most purposes we would want to say that it is true that the face of a child's block is square, that a city block is also, etc. By restricting its attention to a simple dyadic relation between states of affairs and what a person assents to reliabilism has no means of introducing the standards of exactness required to assess truth in such situations.

Even if we could devise a way of measuring a person's success, how high a probability of this success do we require in order to evaluate a belief as rational? Clearly, we must not require uniform success. This would preclude the possibility of there being a justified belief that was in fact false. An object may look red to X and he may believe that it is. If the object is in fact some other color, the background illumination temporarily abnormal, and little is at stake if X's belief were mistaken, then we could correctly say that X held a justified but false belief. To account for such examples defenders of reliabilism only require there to be a "tendency" for X to have correct beliefs in relevantly similar situations. But a "tendency" for success means success with a probability ranging from just over .5 (more often right than wrong) to just under 1 (almost perfect success), and it seems arbitrary to choose any specific probability within this interval. Suppose, for example, that we start from conditions of poor illumination and gradually improve the lighting until it is nearly normal. As we do, we find that X's probability of success increases correspondingly from .55 to .95. At what point do we evaluate a specific belief of X's about the redness of an object as now rational? It would be arbitrary to choose any one number, say .90, over others, say .75 or .55. Yet according to reliabilism, with the information provided by the series of tests we should be able to give an unequivocal assessment of the rationality of a given belief.

The most serious objection to reliabilism is presented, however, by features of perceptual belief that distinguish it from acceptance in a way noted in the previous section. Both 'rational' and 'justified' are normative terms and when applied to belief imply that a belief ought to be held. This in turn presupposes that in some sense whether or not the belief is held is within the control of the agent, that he or she can choose whether to hold it. Now it is just such a feature that seems to be lacking in beliefs as characterized by reliabilism. As we have seen, beliefs are, according to this theory, causal effects of neurophysiological processes, which register environmental states of affairs accurately or inaccurately in a way analogous to the way a thermometer registers temperature. A given type of process will thus be a causally sufficient condition for a belief as its effect. But if this is so, it is difficult to see how a person can choose to have a particular belief, and if there is no choice the evaluative terms 'rational' and 'justified' have no application.

When we look closely at how we evaluate perceptual beliefs in actual situations, we see that it is precisely those features of these beliefs not accounted for by the reliabilist theory that are crucial for their evaluation. That an object looks red to X may be a function of his visual mechanisms and be beyond his control. But whether he accepts an utterance of the descriptive sentence 'This is red' as true would certainly seem to be within X's control. If he is in a dimly lit environment, we expect him to notice this, recognize the increased liability of error, and take precautions against it by scrutinizing the object longer, moving more closely towards it, or perhaps even refusing to assent to any color description until illumination has improved or he has moved to a brighter room. The extent to which X is active in taking these precautions against error will thus determine the rationality of his acceptance, and only so far as his belief is the result of this acceptance would it seem that it also can be characterized as 'rational' or 'irrational'. It is not what happens to him as the passive registering device of reliabilism, but what he does that is crucial in applying the evaluative terms. Moreover, the degree of effort expected would always seem to be assessed relative to the costs of a mistake or to a benefit accruing to a correct belief. If a penalty for mistaken color descriptions or a reward for correct ones is introduced into our test situation, then we would expect greater precautions against error. If nothing is at stake, then the way an object looks to X at first glance may be regarded in itself as a justifiable basis for assent to a particular color description.

So far discussion has been restricted to perceptual beliefs. When we turn to indirect beliefs based on other evidential beliefs, difficulties of a different sort arise. For such beliefs reliabilism postulates what one writer[26] terms "evidentiary mechanisms," which generate hypotheses from evidential beliefs. The reliability or "evidentiary value" of a given cognitive mechanism and the processes by which it produces indirect beliefs will be determined, as before, by its tendency to produce true beliefs. An indirect belief in a hypothesis will be justified if it is the effect of justified evidential beliefs by means of reliable mechanisms. As before, the theory regards the processes produced by these mechanisms as neurophysiological in nature, though their exact nature is unknown to us at present. We can know their reliability, however, so far as we can compare the indirect beliefs they produce with the states of affairs the beliefs represent.

One possible way such comparisons could be made is illustrated by the following example. Suppose we ask our X to now guess the color of the balls in an urn containing 50 balls on the basis of a series of samples of 10 or fewer balls. Each observed sample is the basis for a separate hypothesis about the constitution of the urn. Let us suppose that in each successive trial X infers that the proportion of balls of a certain color in the urn matches that of the observed sample. Thus, on observing the first sample S_1 consisting of 6 balls, 3 red and 3 blue, X believes that the urn consists of balls that are half red and half blue. From a second sample S_2 consisting of 9 balls, 6 red and 3 blue, he infers the ratio of red to blue to be 2:1. From a third sample S_3 of 10 balls, 4 red and 6 blue he infers a ratio of 2:3. And so on for some number n of samples $S_1, S_2, \ldots, S_n$. Let us suppose that after examining all the balls we know that the urn consists of the same number of red and blue balls, and that on the basis of n samples X's beliefs are correct 3 out of 5 times, or that he has a probability of .6 of being correct. From the next sample S_{n+1} X forms still another belief about the urn. Shall we say that his belief is rational based on the reliability of the "evidentiary mechanisms" producing this belief?

The question, along with the assumptions behind it, is, of course, nonsensical. What determines our assessment of rationality is whether X has followed *rules* that *we* accept as governing inferences from samples to populations. X's frequency of success has in itself no bearing on whether this has occurred. It is quite possible that for any finite number n samples X *never* correctly describes the proportion of balls in the urn, though the probability of this occurring diminishes as n increases. Yet though he is never correct, we could still maintain that a given belief was rational because it was inferred from evidence by rules accepted as governing such an inference. Further, X may be correct in his descriptions in a high proportion of cases, and still a given belief may be evaluated as irrational if rules governing the inference from evidence to the description were violated. Unlike the situation for perceptual beliefs, where observations of frequency of success do have some bearing on the reliability of processes, empirical criteria seem to be totally irrelevant to the reliability of the processes or "mechanisms" producing indirect beliefs. The term 'reliability' in this latter context must itself be interpreted in terms of conformity to socially accepted rules of inference, and to this success in itself has no relevance.

Consistent with its general view of belief and justification, reliabilism has proposed a causal condition for justified belief requiring that an indirect belief be causally "sustained" by the evidential beliefs upon which it is based.[27] Suppose again our subject X confronted with sample S_1 of 3 red and 3 blue balls. This evidence then inductively supports the 'Half red, half blue' hypothesis. Suppose that X believes this hypothesis, but not on the basis of his observation of the sample. Instead, an ignorant old man whispers in his ear 'Half red, half blue', and X believes the old man to be a divinely inspired prophet. Then X may believe the hypothesis, and evidence available to him may logically support it. But X's belief in this evidence does not cause his belief in it; the cause is instead the old man's whisper in conjunction with a belief in its divine origins. Hence, it is argued, X is not justified in his belief because the causal sustaining condition has not been fulfilled. Robert Audi in defending this view argues for a distinction between an "impersonal" logical justification for an indirect belief in a hypothesis *h* based on evidence *e* and a "personal" justification for a belief in *h* as caused by belief in *e*. X may be justified in an impersonal, rule-governed sense in believing in *h* on the basis of *e*. But if the belief is not caused by the belief in *e*, Audi contends, it is not *his* justification for holding it. In order for *him* to be justified the causal condition must be satisfied.[28]

There is, of course, an important difference between we as onlookers accepting a hypothesis *h* on the basis of evidence *e* and another person X accepting *h* on the basis of some other evidence *e'*, even though *e* is available to him. Only if X accepts *h* on the same evidential basis as we would, will we evaluate his belief as justified. But to import causal terminology to explain this distinction commits the same error as was criticized above when perceptual beliefs were discussed. When we apply 'justified' or 'rational' to a belief, we assume the belief to be the result of an act of acceptance that could be withheld. To require that a justified belief be the causal effect of evidential beliefs seems inconsistent with this basic feature of our use of the evaluative terms. It is not what has happened to a person and how it has happened that is being evaluated. Instead, it is what he has done and what is within his control. In the case of X's inferring from a sample to a hypothesis about the total population we are, as before for perceptual beliefs, evaluating the extent to which X has taken precautions against error, in this case whether he has thoroughly shaken the urn before drawing the balls or drawn the balls from different areas of the urn in order to insure a random or varied sample. It is thus not the relation between observed sample and belief in h as such that is being evaluated but is instead acceptance of *h* relative to actions taken in selecting the sample. This acceptance is not itself a causal effect of evidential beliefs.

Some may argue that to introduce acts of acceptance is to introduce mysterious mental items incapable of cause-effect explanation by the natural sciences. Any philosophy consistent with the aims of the sciences must therefore reject this introduction. Such an objection, however, fails to recognize what is really at issue. It is not being denied that beliefs can be described as brain states, nor that these brain states are causally related to other brain states, environmental events, and a person's behavior. Nor are acts of acceptance being introduced as mysterious causes of beliefs. The relation between acts of acceptance and belief, we may recall, is the conceptual one between an act and its result, analogous to that between shutting the door and the door being shut. To describe a belief as the result of an act of acceptance is to describe the belief in a certain way, not to characterize it as an effect of a mysterious, nonphysical cause. What is being claimed throughout our criticism of reliabilism is that such a form of description is necessary in order to apply evaluative terms such as 'justified' and 'rational'. For certain purposes causal terminology applied to beliefs may be appropriate, but for the purposes of evaluation it is not. To show why it is inadequate and how its failings are those inherited from assumptions of classical epistemology has been the central aim of this chapter.

This completes our discussion of reliabilism as a theory that states criteria for rational belief in terms of a causal relation between states of beliefs as effects and either environmental states of affairs or other beliefs as causes. We are now free to turn our attention to a theory that states criteria for rational acceptance in terms of a logical relation between propositions. This relation, like the causal relation of reliabilism, also excludes any consideration of individual or social purposes.

Chapter 3

Induction and
Logical Probability

The central topic of this chapter is a cognitivist theory of rational acceptance referred to as "probabilism," a theory that attempts to formulate criteria for the rational acceptance of a hypothesis in terms of a logical relation between the hypothesis and evidence. This relation is one for which increasing evidential support raises the "logical probability" of the hypothesis. Probabilism has not lacked critics. Nevertheless, it remains the most carefully developed attempt to formulate standards for rational acceptance within the cognitivist tradition, and its difficulties reflect those of this tradition in general. There are two variants of the theory. The skeptical variant requires that we have justified certainty in a hypothesis, or that we be able to assign it a logical probability of 1. Since this can never be done for empirical generalizations, acceptance of them can never be justified. The best inquirers can do is assign a logical probability less than 1 and leave the decision whether or not to accept the hypothesis as a basis for actions to those making practical decisions. The nonskeptical variant of the theory maintains that acceptance can be justified and attempts to state rules of acceptance relative to logical probability and related features such as the hypothesis' information content. The last two sections of this chapter (2.4 and 2.5) are devoted to a discussion and criticism of these two variants, with Section 2.4 focusing on Carnap's method for assigning logical probabilities and the last section on a variety of proposed rules of acceptance. The first three sections review some much-discussed features of induction as preliminaries to this criticism and the introduction of the pragmatic alternative in the next chapter. Sections 2.1 and 2.2 outline some central logical features of inductive inferences to uniform generalizations and contrasts rules of inference used in inferring to empirical generalizations to procedural rules used in selecting evidence. The third section outlines some features of inferences from evidence to statistical generalizations that are relevant to assessing Carnap's method of assigning probabilities.

3.1 INDUCTIVE INFERENCES

The basic features of inductive inferences are most easily explained by means of simple examples in which ascriptive generalizations about a population are inferred from descriptions of a limited sample. We observe some finite number n of swans, observe they are all white, and report what we have observed by the observation sentences 'This swan is white', 'That swan is white', etc. On this basis we infer the generalization 'All swans are white'. More generally, from n instances $a_1, a_2, \ldots, a_n$ of a general kind A which all share an attribute B we can infer that all As are B. Using 'Aa_1 & Ba_1' to stand for 'Individual a_1 is both an A and a B' (e.g. 'This is both a swan and white') and '$\forall x(Ax \supset Bx)$' for 'Everything which is an A is a B' or 'All As are B', the form of the inductive inference can be represented symbolically by

$$Aa_1 \ \& \ Ba_1$$
$$Aa_2 \ \& \ Ba_2$$
$$\cdot$$
$$\cdot$$
$$\cdot$$

$$\underline{\underline{Aa_n \ \& \ Ba_n}}$$
$$\forall x(Ax \supset Bx)$$

We shall refer to this as the *ascriptive pattern* of inductive inference. As before for practical inferences (cf. Section 1.2), the double lines indicate that the inference must be nondeductive if the n number of As in the sample is less than the total population of As described by the universal conclusion. In such cases there will always be the logical possibility of the premises being true and the conclusion false. The so-called "problem of induction" first explicitly posed by Hume becomes then that of explaining how, faced with its possible error, we can ever be justified in accepting the conclusion on the basis of accepting its premises. The skeptical view is that the possibility of error makes justified acceptance impossible.

For causal generalizations there is a similar rule of inference. Suppose we are testing to determine whether innoculations of vaccine Y will cure a disease of type Z. We observe after a number of trials that administering Y will cure Z, and hence conclude that the presence of Y is part of the *sufficient condition* of Z's cure. After another sequence of trials we observe that for subjects not receiving the innoculations there is no cure, and conclude that the absence of Y is invariably followed by the absence of Z, or that Y is a *necessary condition* of Z. On the basis of both sequences of trials we can then conclude that Y is both the *necessary condition and part of the sufficient condition* of Z. Let $a_1, a_2, ..., a_n$ be the n occasions at which events of type A (e.g. administering the vaccine Y to subjects) or its absence -A (withholding the vaccine) occur, and let $\phi(A)$ be a complex conjunction of conditions in which A occurs as a factor. If B and -B be types of events which subsequently occur or fail to occur on these occasions, then the form of inference is

$\phi(A)a_1$ & Ba_1
$\phi(A)a_2$ & Ba_2
.
.
.
$\phi(A)a_k$ & Ba_k
-Aa_{k+1} & -Ba_{k+1}
-Aa_{k+2} & -Ba_{k+2}
.
.
.
-Aa_n & -Ba_n

$$\overline{\overline{\forall x[\phi(A)x \supset Bx) \& (-Ax \supset -Bx)]}}$$

The conclusion represents the sentence stating that A is both a part of the complex ϕ as sufficient for B and is necessary for B^1. For this *causal pattern* of inductive inference there is again the possibility of there being a false conclusion inferred from true premises.

Functional correlations of the general form $y = f(x_1, x_2, ..., xn)$, where y is the dependent variable and $x_1, x_2, ..., x_n$ the one or more independent variables, can be regarded as being inferred by an extension of this causal pattern. Quantitative measurements of how changes in an independent variable are accompanied by changes in the dependent variable are the basis for inferring a general functional equation relating the variables.

Philosophers of science have objected to characterizing scientific inquiry as the use of an inductive inference. Instead, they contend, investigators typically first propose a hypothesis, and then proceed to test it by deducing from it consequences that can be compared to what we observe. The hypothesis is falsified if the predicted consequences fail to occur; if they do occur the hypothesis has been given added confirmation. For an ascriptive generalization such as 'All swans are white' the deductive inference will have as premises the generalization and the sentence 'This individual is a swan', while its conclusion will be the prediction 'This will be white'. Its form is thus

$$\forall x(Ax \supset Bx)$$
$$\frac{Aa_1}{Ba_1}$$

where a_1 is any arbitrarily chosen individual. This inference—what is known as a *direct inference*—is deductively valid. Hence, if its conclusion turns out to be in fact false, we know that at least one of its premises is false. Since Aa_1 is an observation sentence that we are normally confident is true, if Ba_1 is false then we normally infer the falsification of the hypothesis $\forall x(Ax \supset Bx)$. If Ba_1 is true, then the hypothesis has received confirmation, though some future instance may still falsify it.

Falsification of an ascriptive generalization normally has two effects. One of them is to lead investigators to restrict the scope of the generalization to a special type of A. Suppose, for example, we find several black swans in Australia. We have then falsified 'All swans are white', but 'All swans in the U. S. and Europe are white' may remain confirmed. In general, for every generalization $\forall x(Ax \supset Bx)$ which is falsified, there is at least potentially some other of the form $\forall x(Ax \;\&\; Cx \supset Bx)$ which remains confirmed, where C is some specifying attribute characterizing a special kind of A. Falsification thus can lead to our substituting a more restricted version of our original generalization. Sometimes, however, we are unaware of any common specifying attribute that will enable survival of falsification, as when we find black swans in Australia, but also an occasional one in a park in England and the United States. In such circumstances the best we can infer is a *statistical generalization* stating a probability that an A is a B, in contrast to the *uniform generalizations* which have so far made up our examples. Our conclusion then becomes 'An A is probably a B' or 'The probability of an A being B is r', where r is some rational number between 0 and 1. The nature of our inference to such statistical generalizations will be our topic in the next section.

The view that scientific inquiry takes the form of proposing and then testing hypotheses rather than generalizing from observations is certainly true at the level of theories. Here it is typical for a theory to be initially proposed as a comprehensive explanation of what had previously been unrelated laws of nature, that is, empirical generalizations that have been terminally accepted as true. Thus, Newton first proposed his gravitational theory as a series of postulates from which could be deductively inferred Galileo's law of acceleration for freely falling bodies in the vicinity of the earth, Kepler's laws of planetary motion, and the motions of the tides. Success in explaining such laws is the basis for the initial provisional acceptance of a theory. It is then subject to testing by deriving from it observable consequences independent of those it was initially proposed to explain. If experimental results coincide with predictions, the theory may itself be terminally accepted as true. If these results do not coincide, then we have a so-called "anomaly" to be explained, either by modifying one or more of the background assumptions employed in deriving and interpreting the result, or by devising a new theory.

Theories are thus not initially inferred from experimental evidence. They are instead proposed through a mode of inference called *retroduction* as an inference to the best explanation of accepted generalizations and possibly also anomolous results confronting predecessor theories.[2] Nevertheless, the relation between subsequent tests in which predictions derived from the theory are compared with observations of experimental outcomes is of the same general logical form as that holding between the singular premises and general conclusions of the ascriptive and causal patterns. The successful passing of an experimental test adds inductive support to a theory, and after a number of such successes it is usually terminally accepted as true, becoming part of the background knowledge of the community of inquirers and performing the functions outlined in Section 1.3.

Advocates of falsificationism follow Popper in claiming that we can falsify a hypothesis, but are never justified in using an inductive inference to conclude that it is true. Instead of adding to the confirmation of a hypothesis *h* through experimental testing, they argue, the most that can be done is to "corroborate" *h*, with the degree of corroboration a function of *h*'s explanatory power and the severity of tests that it survives relative to rival hypotheses.[3] But it is difficult to see the difference between surviving a test designed to attempt to falsify a hypothesis *h* and confirming *h* on the basis of this test. In fact, at some stage we do accept theories as true, and the basis for this acceptance is the experimental evidence obtained from successful tests.[4] In what follows I shall thus ignore falsificationism, concentrating instead on the principal attempt to devise rules for accepting a hypothesis based on the positive support it receives from confirming evidence.

When we turn to empirical generalizations the view that scientific inquiry is hypothesis testing and not generalization from observed data is only partly true. Normally at this level a hypothesis is first proposed on the basis of background knowledge and is of a more general form than that finally accepted after testing. Thus, for an ascriptive generalization we might hypostatize that based on observations of other species there is a positive correlation between swans and the color of their plummage. On examining individual swans we notice that they share the attribute of whiteness and infer the the more specific generalization 'All swans are white'. For a causal generalization the investigator may begin with the hypothesis that a certain general cause produces a given effect. After testing, a correlation may then be inferred between a more specific type of this cause and a more specific effect. For a functional correlation it is common to hypostatize that one type of quantity varies continuously with another, as Galileo guessed that the distance fallen by a freely falling body varies continuously with the time interval of fall prior to measuring specific intervals of distance and time with his inclined plane experiments. The exact functional relation between the two variables will be then projected from the measured values. In all these ways we approach nature by means of general hypotheses as initial guesses, while the answers we eventually elicit by induction are more specific than our initial starting points.

As before for theories, however, these considerations have no bearing whatsoever on the logical relations that hold between singular observation sentences as premises and the generalizations inductively based upon them, since this relation is independent of the particular form that inquiry takes. I shall be referring below to the acceptance of a hypothesis h relative to evidence e. If h is either a theory or empirical generalization, then e will be the set of singular premises from which h is inferred by means of an inductive inference. It is of no concern to us whether e constitutes tests of a previously proposed h or whether h is the result of generalizing or projecting from e. It is important to recognize that the scope of the term 'evidence' as employed here extends only to observational evidence, evidence reported by observation sentences that can be acquired by means of selecting individuals to be described, conducting experimental tests, etc. It does not include, as it does for some writers, background knowledge consisting of laws initially explained by a proposed theory or assumptions used in deriving deductive consequences from hypotheses.[5]

3.2   PROCEDURAL RULES

The ascriptive and causal patterns of inductive inference discussed above can be regarded as rules licensing the inference of a general conclusion from singular premises. As such they are specifications of the following

> *General Rule of Induction:* From singular premises reporting instances exhibiting a pattern we may infer a generalization projecting this pattern on future unobserved instances.

This has been historically stated as the rule that "the future will be like the past." Which particular kind of pattern is projected by the inferred generalization will depend on its form, whether an ascriptive, causal, or functional generalization, or a theory. As has often been pointed out, it is impossible to justify this General Rule of Induction in terms of some higher criterion of rationality. Conformity to the rule is in itself a necessary condition for saying of an empirical inquiry that it is "rational;" any violation is necessarily "irrational."

But while conformity to some version of the General Rule is a necessary condition, it is certainly not sufficient for rationality. Any inductive rule is nondeductive; there will always be the possibility of the premisses being true but the conclusion false. For a person's acceptance of a general conclusion to be evaluated as "rational" or "justified" he must also follow *procedural* or *methodological rules* for selecting evidential premisses in ways that reduce the risk of error. The rational inquirer is one who takes precautions in the specific ways prescribed by the rules. Unlike inductive rules, procedural rules can be justified. We can describe in logical terms specific ways in which true premisses of an inductive inference might lead to a false conclusion. A given procedural rule is justified by showing for one of these ways that if we follow the rule error is less likely.[6] Since procedural rules are applied within the framework of an inductive inference, repeated applications of them can reduce but never eliminate the possibility of error. In this sense the rules are "openended"; there is never any a priori reason for terminating their application. This feature of them we shall find in Chapter 4 to be of considerable importance for our formulation of a pragmatic condition for acceptance.

Which procedural rule is applicable will depend on the type of inductive inference being used.

Ascriptive Generalizations

For inferences to ascriptive generalizations error is due to a possible "bias" in the sample from which a particular conclusion is inferred. Consider a given generalization of the form $\forall x(Ax \supset Bx)$, e.g. 'All swans are white', inferred from the evidence Aa_1 & Ba_1, Aa_2 & Ba_2,..., Aa_n & Ba_n. It is possible that the individuals $a_1, a_2,...,a_n$ of the sample share in common some other attribute C, which is a necessary condition for an A being B. In this case from the sample we could only infer $\forall x(Ax$ & $Cx \supset Bx)$ or 'All As which are C are B', and our original generalization 'All As are B' would be falsified by the first individual a_{n+k} we encounter that is not a C. Thus, if our sample is restricted to North American swans, we would be justified in inferring only 'All North American swans are white', with the possibility remaining that a swan outside North America would be some other color.

Precautions against such a possibility can be taken by varying those attributes of objects of kind A being sampled that are potential necessary conditions for the attribute B. These potential necessary conditions are called *relevant attributes,* and are typically specifications of relevant types or fields of attributes singled out relative to our background knowledge. To vary an object of kind A with respect to a relevant type of attribute is to choose As that differ with respect to that type. Knowledge of other species of birds, for example, may inform us that geographical location, age, and sex are types of attributes relevant to color of plummage, while length of wing span and weight are not. To vary with respect to the types of attributes regarded as relevant on the basis of this background is to choose swans at different geographical locations, ages, and sexes, but to ignore differences in wing span and weight. Let $\alpha_1, \alpha_2, ..., \alpha_m$ be variables standing for m number of relevant attribute types whose n specific attributes are respectively $C_{11}, C_{12}, ..., C_{1n}, C_{21}, C_{22}, ...,$ $C_{2n}, ..., C_{m1}, C_{m2}, ..., C_{mn}$, where a given C_{ij} is the jth specific attribute of the ith attribute type. We then have the following procedural selection rule for ascriptive generalizations.

Ascriptive Variation Rule: For a given generalization of the form $\forall x(Ax \supset Bx)$ to the extent feasible for each known relevant attribute type α_i vary those attributes $C_{i1}, C_{i2}, ..., C_{in}$ which are potentially necessary conditions for an A being a B.

To apply this rule is to choose an A to be included in the sample that is not C_{ij} *for the* jth instance of attribute of type α_i, e.g. choose a swan which lacks the attribute of being from North America as a specific kind of geographical location. If a selected individual A is not C_{ij} and is a B, we have eliminated C_{ij} as a necessary condition for an A being a B and a possible defeator of our generalization.

Notice that the phrase "to the extent feasible" occurs in the formulation of this rule. We may choose to ignore some relevant attribute types because of the difficulty of varying them, as in selecting a sample of swans it may be difficult to determine age. Also, for those relevant attributes we do choose to vary, there may be some, e.g. sex, for which there will be a limited number of instances; a given organism will be either male or female. But for others such as geographical location any partitioning of the field of the attribute into specific attributes is arbitrary and can be replaced by one more specific. Thus, we can distinguish the geographical location of a species of organism with respect to continent, selecting individuals from North America, Eurasia, Africa, Australia, etc. But we can also distinguish location with respect to mountainous regions, plains, deserts, etc., and even specific habitats within these regions. Every finite sample of As will be similar in some respects other than being simply As. There is always the possibility that there may be some attribute C holding of them all that is a necessary condition for B, no matter how specific a partitioning of the relevant fields that we employ. Moreover, even if in principle for a specific partitioning there were a finite number of specific attributes that could be varied, it may be either technically impossible to bring about such a variation or impractical because of its cost. In this respect the Variation Rule is open-ended, always admitting of further applications. Some logicians have constructed inductive logics on the basis of a "Principle of Limited Variety" that postulates that there be a limited number of attributes with respect to which individuals of a population can differ.[7] To claim that the Variation Rule is openended is, in effect, to deny this principle.

The Variation Rule may be difficult and even impossible to apply if our background knowledge is insufficient to isolate relevant types of attributes. As an alternative investigators can employ a *randomizing procedure* designed to make it unlikely that the As selected as sample share in common some attribute C necessary for B. Examples of procedures are shuffling cards before selection, shaking an urn of balls thoroughly prior to drawing a sample, selecting every twentieth name in a phone book for a survey of persons in a given locale, and selecting individuals by using a randomizing device choosing their social security numbers. The larger the sample selected by such a procedure the less likely will it be that it is biased with respect to C. The rule employed can be summarized as the following

Ascriptive Randomizing Rule: For a given generalization $\forall x(Ax \supset Bx)$ select a sample on which it is based as large as is feasible by a randomizing procedure that reduces the probability that members of the sample share an attribute C necessary for B.

A *random* sample is a sample selected on the basis of some randomizing procedure.[8] To increase the size of such a sample to the extent feasible is to employ the traditional "method of simple enumeration" prescribing increases of sample size in order to reduce the possibility of error. Since there is typically no upper limit to sample size, this rule is, like the Variation Rule, also openended.

Whether the Variation or Randomizing Rule is employed will depend on the types of objects being described. Discussions of statistical inferences have historically been dominated by examples of games of chance where the sample is assumed to be one selected by a randomizing procedure. Such a procedure can also be employed when individuals can be labelled or assigned a position in a series, as for social security numbers or position in a phone book. But organisms and inorganic compounds in nature come with no such labels or positions, and for them there is often no alternative to the Variation Rule. Even where the Randomizing Rule can be applied, it must be recognized as possibly yielding mistaken results that could be corrected by the Variation Rule. Suppose an investigator were to survey the inhabitants of a city with regard to income level by selecting names occurring in every hundreth position in the phone book. The conclusion inferred would be distorted because omitted from the survey will be those unable to afford a phone. A more justifiable conclusion will be inferred on the basis of varying possession of a phone as an attribute type relevant to income level. The Randomizing Rule is usually more economical to apply and for this reason is often resorted to. But if background knowledge isolating relevant attribute types is available and variation of potential necessary conditions is feasible, it should play a subsidiary role to the Variation Rule.

Causal Generalizations

Many of the features of procedural rules just outlined can be extended to rules applicable to causal and functional generalizations, and hence our discussion can now be more brief. For causal generalizations the variation rule combines Mill's methods of agreement and difference and is applied to relevant factors. Let $\forall x[(A)x \supset Bx) \,\&\, (-Ax \supset -Bx)]$ be a causal generalization stating that A is a necessary condition for B and part of its sufficient condition ϕ. The variation rule for the sufficiency of A in conjunction with other factors of ϕ is analogous to the Ascriptive Variation Rule. Here it is in the form of Mill's method of agreement prescribing that causal factors $C_{i1}, C_{i2}, ..., C_{in}$ be varied for each relevant causal type α_i in order to insure that no one of them is a necessary condition for the effect B. While varying these factors the event A is repeated in the sequence of trials. The variation rule for the necessity of A is Mill's method of difference prescribing that the relevant causal factors be kept present in the absence of A in order to insure that no one of them is sufficient in the context ϕ for B. Combining these rules we have the following

> *Causal Variation Rule:* For a given causal generalization $\forall x[\phi(A)x \supset Bx) \,\&\, (-Ax \supset -Bx)]$ to the extent feasible for each known relevant causal type α_i vary the specific causal factors $C_{i1}, C_{i2}, ..., C_{in}$ as potentially necessary conditions of B while maintaining A, and maintain $C_{i1}, C_{i2}, ..., C_{in}$ as potentially sufficient conditions of B in the absence of A.[9]

As before, background knowledge will function to isolate relevant types of causes within which more specific causes are distinguished, as light, temperature, and nutrients are known to be relevant to plant growth. Also, since there are indefinitely many specifications of causes, the application of this procedural rule is again openended.

In order to determine whether A as a part of ϕ is a sufficient cause of B a randomizing procedure can in special circumstances be employed to reduce the probability that the presence of some other factor is necessary for B. As before for ascriptive generalizations, this occurs when we are ignorant of specific causal factors relevant to the effect, as occurs when we flip a coin to determine heads or tails or throw a die. In such cases we can determine only the probability of a specific effect. Increasing the number of trials has the effect of increasing the reliability of the conclusion about the probability of the effect we infer from the observed data. For uniform causal generalizations background knowledge is often sufficient to isolate at least some relevant types of causal factors within the investigators control, and the Causal Variation Rule is then employed.

Functional Correlations

The variation rule for functional correlations is similar to that for causal generalizations. For a correlation of the form $y = f(x_1, x_2, ..., x_n)$ we now interpret $\alpha_1, \alpha_2, ..., \alpha_m$ to be other variables besides $x_1, x_2, ..., x_n$ on which y might depend. We thus vary these variables as potential necessary conditions of variations in the dependent variable y and maintain them in the absence of $x_1, x_2, ..., x_n$ as potential sufficient conditions of y.

Functional correlations also introduce features requiring an additional procedural rule. The dependent and independent variables of these correlations range over a continuum of real numbers that can only be approximated by any value read from a scale of measurement and stated in terms of a rational number. For each such value there will invariably be some interval of possible error that will depend on the precision of the measuring instrument. Thus, the length of objects will vary continuously, but any individual object will have a specific measured value that we can state within an interval of possible error. Measured with an ordinary ruler the length of an object may be 10.4 ± .25 centimeters; measured with an instrument employing a calibrated microscope the same object may be described as having a length of 10.4137 ± .0025 centimeters. When an investigator projects a general functional correlation from correlations between a series of measured values there is inevitably a potential source of error introduced by the inaccuracy of measurements within a given interval of error.

Precautions against this source of error can normally be accomplished by introducing a more precise measuring instrument or being more careful in employing those instruments available. We thus have the following

Functional Precision Rule: For a functional generalization of the form $y = f(x_1, x_2, ..., x_n)$ decrease to the extent feasible the interval of possible error by increasing the precision of measurements for the values of y and $x_1, x_2, ..., x_n$.

Like the other procedural rules, this is also openended. Reducing the interval of error to zero is a limit that we can approach in varying degrees but never reach. The extent to which it is approached will depend on what is technically possible at a given time and on practical considerations of the sort to be discussed in the next chapter.

Theories

The paradigm scientific theories are those of physics, and these are usually stated as differential equations as more abstract forms of functional correlations. In the testing of a theory the Functional Precision

Rule is applicable as a means of avoiding the kind of error just discussed. Historically the falsification of a theory has often occurred when a more precise means is introduced for measuring phenomena the theory had successfully explained when less precisely measured, as the Ptolemaic model of the solar system was falsified when a more accurate means of determining the positions of the planets was made possible by the introduction of the telescope. In addition, a form of variation rule is employed when theories are tested relative to phenomena different from those it was initially introduced to explain. Popper has emphasized that sheer repetition of successful tests is an insufficient basis for acceptance of a theory. The tests must also be "stringent," that is, employ as precise a means of measurement as is currently available and be made relative to different types of phenomena.[10] Einstein's theory of gravitation was initially proposed as an explanation of all the laws of nature previously explained by Newton's theory plus the anomaly presented to this theory by the precession of the perihelion of Mercury. But it was accepted only after it successfully predicted the deflection of light rays from a star under the influence of the gravitational field of the sun and the displacement of the spectral lines of light from dense stars towards the red, novel phenomena that the theory had not explained when it was initially introduced.

3.3. STATISTICAL INFERENCES.

So far we have been discussing only inductive inferences to uniform generalizations where in the samples or trials described by the premises an attribute or effect is invariably present. We now turn to *statistical inferences,* inferences to statistical generalizations stating probabilities of an attribute or effect on the basis of premises describing their relative frequency of occurrence. Here our discussion will be limited to ascriptive and causal generalizations; statistical functional correlations introduce special difficulties that are irrelevant to the evaluation of the cognitivist theory considered in the next two sections.

One standard rule known as the *Straight Rule* licenses inferences to a statistical generalization projecting the probability of an attribute or effect directly from an observed relative frequency. For an ascriptive generalization the inference has a premiss stating that for a sample of n individuals $a_1, a_2, ..., a_n$ of kind A m number of them have attribute B, or that the relative frequency or proportion of As which are B is some fraction m/n. The probability of an A being a B for the entire population of As is then inferred to be this same fraction. As for uniform generalizations, we can also regard the statistical generalization as a hypothesis that is being tested in accordance with the Straight Rule relative to the frequency observed in the sample. The form of the inference is as follows:

For sample $a_1, a_2, ..., a_n$ the relative frequency of *A*s
which are *B* is m/n

The probability of an *A* being a *B* is m/n.

We would be using this rule if we inferred from a sample of 100 persons in which 25 were left-handed to the conclusion that the probability of a human being left-handed is 1/4.[11] The ascriptive pattern of inductive inference stated at the beginning of Section 3.1 can be regarded as a special case of this inference in which $m = n$, and hence $m/n = 1$. For causal statistical generalizations the premiss will report that for *n* trials the relative frequency of effect *B* given events of type *A* is some fraction m/n. The conclusion is that the probability of *B* given *A* is this same fraction, or $p(B/A) = m/n$. Again, the uniform causal generalization $\forall x[\phi(A)x \supset Bx]$ stating that *A* is a part of the sufficient condition for *B* will be the special case in which $p[B/\phi(A)] = 1$.

The Straight Rule is applicable in many situations, and is widely employed in scientific inquiry. But there are situations in which we would be unwilling to accept the conclusion it yields. Consider, for example, 10 trials in which a coin is tossed and turns up heads on 8 occasions. The relative frequency of heads for the trials is then $\frac{4}{5}$, and by the Straight Rule we would infer that the probability of this coin turning up heads when tossed is $\frac{4}{5}$ or .8 and that the coin is therefore biased. If from a large sample of other coins we find $\frac{9}{10}$ are unbiased, then we might initially estimate that the probability of this particular coin being unbiased is .9 and that it is therefore very likely to turn up heads on half of any sequence of tosses. This is the assignment of what is known as a *prior probability* to the hypothesis of unbias. If this were the probability, then any sub-sequence of tosses, including our 10 tosses, could diverge from an even ratio of heads to tails, and we would discount the relative frequency in our small number of trials. But if we were to toss the coin 100 times and still observe $\frac{4}{5}$ to be heads, we would weight the observed relative frequency more heavily in our assignment of probability, and as the number of trials is indefinitely increased the relative frequency would "overwhelm" or cancel our initial estimate of the coin's lack of bias. In such situations where we can assign an initial or prior probability, then, the probability inferred as conclusion, what is known as the *posterior probability*, will be a function of this prior probability, the observed relative frequency, and the number of trials.

These considerations can be summarized by stating the general form of the rule used to infer a probability conclusion from an observed relative frequency *r* when a prior probability r' can be estimated.

The prior probability of $p(B/A)$ being $x = r'$
For n trials the relative frequency of B
   given A is r

The posterior probability of $p(B/A)$ being $x = f(r',r,n)$

In our example $x = 1/2$ or .5 and the prior probability r' of heads relative to a toss being .5 (the coin being unbiased) is .9, while the relative frequency r for the 10 trials is .8. The conclusion states that the probability of B given A is a function of r', r, and n, without specifying this function. This should be regarded as a general outline, with specific rules generated by specifying the function f. We shall refer to this as the *Generalized Bayesian Rule* after the theorem in the probability calculus called "Bayes' Theorem" used to calculate specific posterior probabilities.[12] As the number of trials n becomes indefinitely large and approaches infinity the posterior probability of $p(B/A)$ being x will be uniquely determined by the value r of the relative frequency. Where $n = 0$ and there is no observed relative frequency, the probability of $p(B/A)$ equalling x is the prior probability r'. Where prior probabilities cannot be assigned and we cannot assert the first premiss, the rule reduces to the Straight Rule for which $p(B/A)$ in the conclusion is equal to r.

The employment of the Generalized Bayesian Rule thus requires an ability to assign prior probabilities. On what basis is this to be done? There are three alternative answers that have been proposed that coincide with the three principal interpretations of probabilities.

Subjective Interpretation

For the subjective or personalist theory probabilities are measures of the degrees of belief that persons have in propositions. These degrees of belief are in turn measured by the odds that persons are willing to accept on a bet that the belief turns out to be true.[13] Applied to the Bayesian Rule this interpretation would assign prior probabilities on the basis of the strength of a person's belief as a subjective psychological state. But the Bayesian Rule is a normative rule prescribing the form of the conclusion that a person *should* accept given certain premises, and for this what a person happens to believe, no matter how irrational the basis, would seem to be irrelevant. A person may be totally convinced that a coin will invariably turn up heads on the basis of what he claims to be divine inspiration. But such a conviction can have no weighting relative to our assignment of a probability to a coin turning up heads relative to an observed relative frequency.

Defenders of the subjective theory often point to the lack of statistical data on which to base assessments of probabilities, claiming that in such cases we must resort to estimates of degrees of belief. But this confuses these estimates with the estimation of relative frequencies that we must often make on the basis of incomplete data. When dark clouds appear overhead my past experience has been that it usually rains. I have not, however, actually counted the proportion of past instances of dark clouds followed by rain, nor do I know of any statistical studies that would provide relative frequencies. Still, in the absence of past relative frequencies it would seem reasonable to make a rough estimate of them, estimating, for example, the relative frequency of rain following dark clouds as about .7, and using this estimate to assign a probability. This probability is not merely expression of a degree of belief, since it has its basis in past experience.

A Priori Interpretation

According to the classical theory of LaPlace probabilities of the form $p(B/A)$ are assigned relative to the number of possible alternatives excluded by B. By what is known as the "Principle of Indifference" alternatives are assumed to be equiprobable if there is no basis for assigning to them different probabilities. Thus, for a throw of a die there are six alternative outcomes. The probability of any one of them, say the occurrence of a five, will be ⅙ in the absence of any evidence to the contrary. For a coin there are two alternatives, heads or tails. Hence, by the Principle of Indifference we assign the probability of a coin turning up heads the value ½. Since prior probabilities are by definition probabilities posited in the absence of relative frequencies that might provide evidence that alternatives are not equiprobable, they can be assigned, according to the a priori interpretation, by this principle.

The Principle of Indifference has been frequently criticized, and for good reasons.[14] To argue that because we do not know that alternatives are not equiprobable we can assume that they are is to commit the fallacy of an argument *ad ignorantium*. In fact, assignment of prior probabilities does not seem to be made on the basis of this principle, but instead on observed structural symmetries. It is because the coin seems evenly balanced that we assign heads an initial probability of ½. A five has a prior probability of ⅙ because the die under consideration does not seem to be loaded. For the games of chance that were the basis for the a priori theory there is invariably information about the structure of their set-up, e.g. the fact that there are 52 cards in a well-shuffled deck of which ¼ are hearts, that there are the same number of red and green balls in an urn which has been well shaken, etc. It is relative to this kind of information, not the mere number of possible alternatives, which determines the assignment of prior probabilities.

Frequency Interpretation

For the frequency theory the only basis for assigning probabilities is observed relative frequencies. If we are able to assign a prior probability to an outcome, therefore, there must be some wider second-level or "covering" statistical generalization based on an observation of a relative frequency from which it can be derived. Thus, to assign a prior probability to this particular coin turning up heads requires there having been a statistical generalization inferred from observations of the relative frequency in which other coins have turned up heads. If coins in general have turned up heads with a frequency of approximately ½, then we can infer that this coin will also, even though we have not previously tested it. This can now be the basis for assigning this coin its prior probability in order to apply the Bayesian Rule. In inferring from a wider statistical generalization about objects of type A to the probability of an outcome for a particular object a_i we assume that there are no relevant differences between a_i and those As used in inferring the generalization. This assumption raises problems involving direct inferences to be discussed in the next section.

We have concluded that the subjective interpretation can be ruled out as a basis for assigning prior probabilities, since what a person happens to believe is irrelevant to what he should accept. But what of the other two so-called "objectivist" interpretations? Actual practice seems to indicate that both interpretations are employed. For games of chance where structural symmetries can be determined the a priori interpretation can be used to assign prior probabilities. In areas of scientific investigation where background knowledge exists in the form of second-level statistical generalizations the frequency interpretation is usually applied. Where neither interpretation can be applied and observed relative frequencies are either unavailable or cannot even be roughly estimated, we must concede there to be no rational basis for inferring a statistical generalization.

So far our discussion has been restricted to inductive rules for inferring statistical generalizations from evidence. As before for uniform generalizations, these rules are not deductive rules: it is possible for the premises in the inferences to which they are applied to be true and the conclusions false. Consider an investigator, for example, attempting to determine the incidence of lung cancer in the population of a city by sampling customers at a tobacco store. Three out of five in this sample may be found to have lung cancer. But surely this is not a reasonable basis for inferring that the probability of an inhabitant of the city having cancer is .6. The customers of the tobacco store would all smoke cigarettes, cigars, or pipes and be in an advanced age group, and we know the probability of cancer relative to these attributes is much higher than for the general population. In general, if C is an attribute relevant to the presence of B, as smoking is relevant to cancer, then the probability of individuals of kind A which are C being B, or $p(B/A\&C)$, may be different from $p(B/A)$. If we conclude that $p(B/A) = r$ from a sample all sharing the attribute C, then we may therefore be mistaken. Compliance with an inductive rule will be again a necessary condition for the acceptance of a statistical generalization relative to evidence. But as examples of the kind just cited show, it is surely not a sufficient condition. Procedural rules are, as before, required to prescribe how the sample is to be selected or the trials conducted in order that this potential source of error not be present. For our example background knowledge would isolate smoking and age as relevant types of attributes, and the Variation Rule would prescribe a choice of sample for which these were varied.

Expositions of the frequency interpretation of the formal probability calculus invariably postulate as evidence a random sample selected by what we can call an "ideal randomizing rule," a rule, which when applied in the long run will yield a sample in which any relevant attribute C will occur with the same frequency as in the whole population. With the assumption of such a rule only the sheer number of instances is relevant to the acceptance of a generalization. We are thus employing the method of simple enumeration, as explained in the previous section. But we can never know whether we are employing such a rule, since any randomizing procedure may be in fact biased towards the attribute C. Kyburg notes how a given random selection procedure may be biased relative to some inferences but not others. Suppose our investigator is a sociologist selecting a sample of college students by first letter of last name on the basis of a drawing from a bag of balls labelled with 26 letters and using the letter drawn for selection. Then this would be a randomizing rule relative to determining students' sexual habits. But if the sociologist draws the letter M from the bag and concludes from his sample that 62% of students are of Scotch ancestry or 100% have last names beginning with M, his generalizations, Kyburg points out, would be worthless.[15] Moreover, they would remain worthless no matter how large the sample, even if it became indefinitely large by repeating the procedure on successive generations of students. As before for uniform generalizations, devising a suitable randomizing procedure will thus depend on isolating relevant attributes provided by background knowledge.

Reichenbach has argued that variation rules such as Mill's methods of agreement and difference are irrelevant to the logic of induction. Instead, all induction is by simple enumeration in which sample size alone is relevant.[16] Variation rules, Reichenbach argues, depend on background knowledge to isolate relevant variables, and this will invariably be established by previous inductions to second-level generalizations that will employ the method of simple enumeration, as when we determine that age is relevant to incidence of cancer. To vary members of a sample with respect to age will be simply to apply the outcome of a previous simple enumeration in which sample size is the only consideration.

There are two difficulties with this argument. One lies with its assumption that inductions to second-level generalizations must be by simple enumeration. If this generalization is part of science, it will almost invariably be established by an application of a variation rule. Of course, there may be a third-level generalization that now determines the variation of this second-level, and a fourth-level determining the third. But this regress to higher generalizations must eventually terminate in some generalization inferred on the basis of a variation rule. The second difficulty is that it assumes that background knowledge will itself determine the extent to which relevant attributes are to be varied. This is not generally the case. Suppose that previous inductions have informed us that age is relevant to the incidence of cancer. This would still only establish that age is a general type of relevant attribute and leave undecided which specific age groups are to be varied in selecting a sample. There may be also previous inductions establishing correlations for specific age groups, e.g. the 35–45 age group, the 45–55 group, etc. But this will now leave indeterminate which specific ages within these groups are to be varied. In general, background knowledge normally establishes types or ranges to be varied, but does not determine the degree of specificity of variation within these ranges. We must conclude, therefore, that variation as well as randomizing rules must usually be applied to inferences to statistical generalizations, certainly to those found in the empirical sciences, if not to those applicable to games of chance. Where variation rules are applicable sample size or number of trials is not in itself an adequate basis for determining whether acceptance or a generalization relative to evidence is justified.

This concludes this brief review of some basic features of inductive inferences and the procedural rules employed in selecting their premises. We should now have a sufficient background to discuss and evaluate the concept of logical probability that has been used in an attempt to establish standards of rational acceptance.

3.4 LOGICAL PROBABILITY AND PROBABLISM

The concept of *logical probability* is introduced to explain the sense of 'probable' that seems to be used when we say such things as 'What he says is probably true' or 'The evidence makes the hypothesis highly probable'. The term 'probable' in the "objectivist" interpretations given by the frequency and a priori theories is applied to events and states of nature. In contrast, logical probability is applied by its advocates to the logical relation between one proposition and others reporting evidence upon which this proposition is based. Applied in this way it is claimed to prescribe the degree of belief that a person should hold in a proposition *p* or the degree to which it is rational to believe it. In Kyburg's words, "We are rational when we believe that which is warranted by the evidence;

and in particular we are rational when we have a *degree* of belief in a given statement...which is precisely that degree justified by the evidence."[17] To be justified in being certain in a proposition p is to assign it a logical probability of 1. To be justifiably certain that it is false is to assign it the value of 0. Other degrees of justified belief will be rational numbers ranging in the interval between 0 and 1.

The view that rational belief can be measured by probability values has been labelled *probabilism*. An initial difficulty with this view should be apparent from our discussion in Section 2.3 of the contrast between belief and acceptance. There it was noted that belief as such is involuntary and that only what is voluntary and within our control can be evaluated as "rational." A belief in a proposition *p* is within our control in so far as it is related to the acceptance of *p*, either as the initial acceptance resulting in the belief in *p* or a decision to accept it in the light of further evidence. But acceptance does not itself admit of degrees; it is all-or-nothing. So far as belief does admit of degrees, therefore, it does not seem capable evaluation as "rational," but without such degrees there can be no assignment of probability values of the kind advocated by probabilism.

Difficulties of a more technical kind become apparent when we turn to the methods devised by Carnap for assigning specific probability values to propositions relative to evidence.[18] Suppose a random sample of 100 individuals out of which 25 are left-handed. Then by one method discussed by Carnap we could assign to the hypothesis that the next individual will be left-handed the logical probability of ¼. Alternatively, ¼ can be said to be the *degree of confirmation* or the "credance value" of the hypothesis *h* that the next individual is left-handed relative to the observed relative frequency in the sample as evidence *e*. The function assigning a probability to a hypothesis about the next individual that is equal to frequency in the sample is analogous to the Straight Rule discussed in the previous section used in inferring from observed relative frequencies to statistical generalizations. Let us represent this *straight rule function* by c^s. Then if *r* is the observed relative frequency in the sample of the occurrence of an attribute *B* for individuals of type *A*, the logical probability of the next *A* selected being a *B* is given by the equation $c^s(h/e) = r$.

Carnap rejects on logical grounds the straight rule function as a measure of degrees of confirmation. Let us suppose that in our sample of 100 individuals all of them happen to share the attribute of having two kidneys. Then the c^s function would assign to the hypothesis that the next individual will have two kidneys the probability of 1. But this would mean that we would be justified in being certain that this hypothesis is true, and Carnap argues that for no contingent, empirical proposition is such certainty warranted. Only if the evidence *e* logically entails the hypothesis *h* should we be able to assign to *h* relative to *e* the value 1, and hence be justifiably certain of it. This would occur if *h* were a logical tautology (a tautology is entailed by any premisses), but not for any contingent hypothesis.

As an alternative to c^s Carnap proposes a function c^*, which assigns probability values to *h/e* relative to the *prior logical probability* of *h* in addition to the relative frequency in *e*. This prior probability we represent again by r'. The prior logical probability of a proposition is determined by the ratio of the possible interpretations (or possible worlds) in which it is true to the totality of possible interpretations. This fraction r' will be inversely proportional to the logical information of the proposition. A tautology such as 'It is raining or it is not raining' of the form $A \vee -A$ has a prior logical probability of 1, since the number of possible interpretations of its constituent sentence 'It is raining' in which it is true is equal to its possible interpretations as either true or false. It thus conveys no logical information and is "empty" of content. A contradiction of the form $A \& -A$ will have the prior value of 0, since it is false for all interpretations. It conveys maximal content. Every contingent proposition will have some rational number value in the interval between 1 and 0. Thus, for $A \vee B$, $r' = \frac{3}{4}$, since for the four possible interpretations of *A* and *B* it is only false when *A* and *B* are false. Every simple singular proposition expressed by a sentence *A*, e.g. 'It is raining' or 'The next individual will be left-handed', will have a prior logical probability of ½. For a conjunction $A \& B$, $r' = \frac{1}{4}$, since it is true only for the one interpretation where *A* and *B* are both true.[19] Thus, the more possible interpretations excluded by a proposition the higher its logical information and the less we are warranted in initially expecting it to be true.

Carnap intends these prior logical probabilities to play the same role as the prior probabilities used in applying the Generalized Bayesian Rule of the previous section. This is evident from his maintaining that the degree of confirmation $c^*(h/e)$ will equal the prior logical probability of *h* where there is no evidence *e* in the form of relative frequencies. As the number of individuals *n* in the sample indefinitely increases, the observed relative frequency *r* begins to dominate over the prior logical probability r'. Hence, as *n* approaches infinity $c^*(h/e)$ approaches to *r*. Where all members of the sample share an attribute *B* the degree of confirmation of the hypothesis that the next individual will be *B* approaches but never equals 1 as the size of the sample approaches infinity. Carnap's c^* thus determines logical probability to be a function of r', *r*, and *n* in a manner analogous to the way posterior probabilities are calculated by applying the Generalized Bayesian Rule. The innovation lies only in the use of logical information to assign prior probabilities.

So far we have been discussing only methods for assigning degrees of confirmation to singular hypotheses. Hintikka has also devised a method that will assign prior logical probabilities to uniform generalizations of the form $\forall x(Ax \supset Bx)$ in order to calculate posterior probabilities.[20] Assigning to uniform generalizations prior logical probabilities requires identifying constituents in terms of which possible interpretations can be listed. These are called *existence-constituents*. For a generalization of the form $\forall x(Ax \supset Bx)$ with two predicates A and B there are four such constituents: $\exists x(Ax \& Bx)$, $\exists x(Ax \& -Bx)$, $\exists x(-Ax \& Bx)$, and $\exists x(-Ax \& -Bx)$.[21] The prior logical probability of a given generalization is now equal, as before, to the ratio of its logical width, the number of interpretations of these constituents under which it is true, to the total number of possible interpretations. For a logical tautology such as one of the form $\forall x(Ax \lor -Ax)$ the prior logical probability r' will be 1; for a contradiction, e.g., $\forall x(Ax \& -Ax)$, $r' = 0$. For all contingent generalizations the values will again be in the interval between 1 and 0. For a uniform generalization of the form $\forall x(Ax \supset Bx)$ (e.g. 'All humans have two kidneys') $r' = \frac{1}{2}$, since it is true under half of the 16 possible interpretations of its four existence-constituents. Carnap's confirmation function can now be adopted to assign degrees of confirmation to uniform generalizations relative to these prior probabilities, evidence consisting of a sample of n As which are all B, and the number n individuals in the sample. Where $n = 0$, the degree of confirmation of h/e equals r'; as n is indefinitely increased this value approaches to $r = 1$. As Hintikka concedes, for statistical generalizations where the observed relative frequency is less than 1 no assignment of degrees of confirmation is possible.

A look at some examples shows this project of assigning prior probabilities in terms of logical information yields very implausible results. In fact, *all* uniform generalizations of the form $\forall x(Ax \supset Bx)$ and *all* singular hypotheses express the same logical content, and hence have the same prior logical probability. The methods just discussed assign all of them the probability of $\frac{1}{2}$, and hence are useless for making crucial distinctions between them. Thus, the generalizations 'All who dance at this disco are young' and 'All who dance at this disco are between the ages of 16 and 18' are uniform generalizations of the same logical form and hence have the same probability of $\frac{1}{2}$. Yet it is obvious that we would regard the latter as conveying more information, and hence being less likely to be true than the former. Similar considerations hold for the singular sentences 'This dancer is young' and 'This dancer is between the ages of 16 and 18'. Both are of the same logical form and have for Carnap the prior probability of $\frac{1}{2}$. But it is again obvious that the latter is initially more improbable than the former.

What such examples show is that it is not the logical content of a sentence that determines our initial assessment of probabilities, but instead the semantic content expressed by its predicate. This semantic information content is in turn determined by the number of possible alternatives excluded. The predicate 'young' excludes only 'old' and perhaps also 'middle-aged'. The predicate '16 to 18 years old', on the other hand, excludes an entire range of three-year intervals, e.g. 13 to 15, 19 to 21, 22 to 24, etc. But such exclusion of alternative possibilities we saw to be precisely the criterion used in the assignment of prior probabilities under the a priori interpretation of probabilities. Switching the criteria from those used in standard statistical inferences that were discussed in the previous section thus produces much less plausible probability assignments.

In fact, the switch is but an elaborate smoke screen whose principal effect is to disguise the fact that the Straight and Bayesian Rules are readily available as means of deriving all the principal formal conclusions derived within the framework of the logical interpretation of probability. Consider again the sample of 100 individuals, 25 of whom are left-handed. We can infer that the next 101st individual has a probability of ¼ of being left-handed from the proportion having this attribute in the sample. Such an inference, however, is indirect, requiring first the application of the Straight Rule to infer from the proportion in the sample to the statistical generalization that the probability of a person being left-handed is ¼, and then the inference from this generalization to the probability for the next individual. In general, if a proportion of the As in a sample of n individuals that are B is m/n, then we can infer first by the Straight Rule that $p(B/A)$ = m/n. Then we can employ a *statistical direct inference* to infer that the $n + $1st A will be a B with probability m/n. The form of this direct inference is

$p(B/A)$ = m/n based on sample $a_1, a_2, ..., a_n$
a_{n+1} is an A
_____
The probability of a_{n+1} being B is m/n.

Thus, the probability of a single individual being B is inferred by the standard Straight Rule plus a direct inference in a manner analogous to the way singular probabilities are assigned by Carnap's c^s function. If the Bayesian Rule were used to infer the first premiss of the direct inference, then we could infer a singular conclusion in a manner analogous to the assignment produced by Carnap's c^* function, but without the implausibilities we have just seen to be introduced by his use of logical width in the assignment of prior probabilities.

Defenders of probabilism have consistently criticized the frequency theory for being unable to apply probability measures to individual events. Kyburg, for example, contends that for this theory the term 'probability' is used only to make "a conjecture about a mass phenomenon" but "never to an individual event." This, he claims, is inconsistent with our ordinary use of the term 'probability' when we say that it will probably rain tomorrow or that the next toss of this coin has a probability of ½ of being heads. There is an important difference between reference to tomorrow's rain and the next toss and reference to simply rain-in-general or a toss of the coin, but this is a distinction, it is argued, the frequency theory is unable to make. Instead, the theory must either dismiss singular probability sentences as meaningless, or as but disguised forms of statistical generalizations referring to general types of events.[22] In contrast, it is claimed that the concept of logical probability does allow us to refer to individual events, and to this extent it has the advantage.

This criticism has absolutely no force, however, as an argument for probabilism. In the first place, logical probabilities are assigned to propositions, not individual events, and the assignment relies on relative frequencies of *types* of events. But second, the frequency theory can allow us to refer to the probability of an individual event as derived by way of a direct inference from a statistical generalization and a premiss asserting that the individual is an instance of the class of individuals referred to by the generalization. The frequency theory makes the entirely plausible claim that the only basis for the assertion of an individual probability is the premisses of such a direct inference. Since assignments of logical probability are based on precisely the same information as expressed by such premisses, the advocates of probabilism are insisting on a distinction in interpretations of individual probabilities without a difference. The situation remains unchanged when prior probabilities, however they are assigned, are introduced, and we infer to the first premiss of a direct inference by using the Bayesian Rule. Here we can again infer to an individual probability. The fact that probabilism assigns prior probabilities in terms of logical information, even supposing (what I have denied) that this is plausible, does not alter the fundamental logical bases for assigning an individual probability. For probabilism the information used for such an assignment will be exactly that expressed by the premisses of a direct inference.

As has often been pointed out, a direct inference from a statistical generalization differs in important ways from one whose premiss is a uniform generalization. Having accepted 'All As are B' and 'Individual a_i is an A', we have no alternative but to accept 'a_i is a B'. The conclusion follows because from 'All As are B' we can infer 'All As that are C are B' for any attribute C. The fact that a special attribute holds of the individual a_i thus does not prevent our deductively inferring the conclusion. But the corresponding inference from $p(B/A) = r$ to $p(B/A\&C) = r$ is invalid, as we have seen. Individual probabilities can be assigned in many ways depending on the attributes holding of the individual being referred to, and there will be alternatives to 'The probability of a_i being B is r' when it is inferred from the relevant statistical generalization. Thus, if Jones is an individual selected from the general population, we might infer from a statistical generalization referring to this population the conclusion 'The probability of Jones developing lung cancer is .12'. But if we know that Jones is a cigarette smoker, then based on statistical surveys of smokers we might conclude that Jones' probability of lung cancer is .65. If we also know that Jones is a coal miner and relevant statistics are available, then the probability may be raised to some rational number such as .85. In general, let $p(B) = r$ be the probability of an individual a_i as a member of the class A (e.g. the class of humans) having the attribute B (e.g. incurring lung cancer) as derived from $p(B/A) = r$. Then there is also the possibility that a_i has n other attributes $C_1, C_2, ..., C_n$ for which $p(B/A\&C_1\&C_2\&...\&C_n) \neq r$. In such a case the probability of a_i being B is also not equal to r.

This is known as the "problem of the reference class," and Reichenbach has stated the way it is solved in practice. We must, he says, choose the narrowest reference class for which a relevant statistical generalization is available in deriving individual probabilities.[23] If no statistical information is available about the frequency of B for the class of individuals which are both A and C, but information is available for the As, then we must base our conclusion about the probability of a_i being B on the generalization $p(B/A) = r$. If statistical information is available about persons who smoke but not for coal miners, then we must conclude that Jones's probability of cancer is that for smokers, i.e. .65. Of course, if it is sufficiently important to be able to predict with more exactness the probability of cancer for Jones, other statistical surveys could be conducted for attributes holding of him, e.g. for being a coal miner, for being of Scotch heritage, for having parents with a history of cancer, etc. In such a case we would withhold, if practically feasible, our assent to the individual probability until this further information is acquired and the reference class suitably narrowed. But if time or resources were limited, as for the physician who must decide immediately whether or not to prescribe a drug for Jones, the individual probability would undoubtedly be accepted based on the wider reference class for which information is presently available. In such a case to accept the conclusion of the direct inference would then also require accepting the proposition that individual a_{n+1} does not differ from the sampled As in any respect that would significantly alter its probability of being a B.

Again, it is important to note that these difficulties of direct inferences apply also to probabilism's assignment of degrees of confirmation to singular hypotheses on the basis of relative frequencies in a sample.[24] To infer that the singular hypothesis has a probability that is identical with the relative frequency in the sample is to make exactly the same assumption that a_{n+1} does not differ from the members of this sample in any way affecting the inferred probability.

In conclusion, then, the argument that probabilism can alone account for individual probabilities is baseless. Such probabilities can be accepted as true as conclusions of direct inferences, and this acceptance can be evaluated as reasonable in the same manner as for any other proposition. What is unique about direct inferences is only the choices they present in selecting their premises, choices influenced by the available information and the feasibility of possibly delaying acceptance until more complete information becomes available. Further, the method by which logical probabilities are assigned to singular hypotheses is virtually the same as that used in inferring to individual probabilities by direct inferences from statistical generalizations. Where novelties are introduced by probabilism, as in its use of logical information to measure prior probabilities, it only manages to generate its most implausible results.

3.5 RULES OF ACCEPTANCE

These technical difficulties are only symptomatic of more fundamental philosophic ones that become apparent when we examine probabilism's attempts to state criteria for rational acceptance. Within probabilism we can distinguish two general ways of approaching this problem, one skeptical, the other nonskeptical. The skeptical advocates of probabilism deny that we are ever justified in accepting an empirical hypothesis as true because this acceptance fails to satisfy a version of the certainty condition. Nonskeptical versions of probabilism, in contrast, concede that acceptance can be justified, and attempt to state criteria for this acceptance based on assigned degrees of confirmation and perhaps other features of hypotheses.

The skepticism typical of the empiricist tradition has been more restricted than the universal skepticism outlined above in Section 2.2. Universal skepticism concludes, as we saw there, that no form of knowledge is possible because we can never have justified absolute certainty in any proposition. Empiricists have instead conceded that we can be justifiably certain of, and hence know, logical tautologies and deductive relations between premises and conclusions. Many empiricists have also claimed that we can also be justifiably certain of propositions describing sensations, e.g. 'This looks red'. Some have even conceded that we can know propositions about individual objects, e.g. that this rose is red. But all versions of classical empiricism following Locke and Hume deny that we can justifiably be certain of any empirical generalization not entailed by observational premises, including all those of the empirical sciences, both uniform and statistical. Nor can we be certain of, and hence know, any singular proposition derivable as a prediction from an empirical generalization, e.g. that the sun will rise tomorrow, that this pencil will fall if released, that the water in this pond will freeze if the temperature falls below 0°C, etc. Without certainty in either empirical generalizations or singular predictions inferred from them we have insufficient grounds for accepting them as true. What we can only justifiably accept are assignments of probabilities, e.g. that the sun will *probably* rise, the pencil *probably* fall, and the pond *probably* freeze.

Carnap's formulations of probabilism clearly show that his primary reason for devising his measures of degrees of confirmation is his adherence to this form of restricted skepticism. Inductive reasoning leading to a conclusion should lead, Carnap says, "not to acceptance or rejection, but to the assignment of a number to a proposition, viz., its c-value" (its degree of confirmation).[25] The reason why we cannot rationally infer to acceptance or rejection is that we lack knowledge as defined by the classical certainty condition. He asks us to consider a situation in which an investigator X is presented with a random sample of 80 Chicagoans of whom 60 share an attribute B. X can draw two conclusions from this sample. One is that the probability of a Chicagoan being *B* is .75. This, Carnap says, cannot be a guide to action because it is "not known to X as long as his knowledge is restricted to the evidence *e* concerning the eighty observed individuals," and only what is known should guide action. The second conclusion is that the logical probability of the next Chicagoan being *B* relative to the evidence presented by the sample is .75. This conclusion may be deductively inferred from *e*, and is hence certain and known.[26] It is on these grounds that Carnap chooses to substitute logical probabilities applied to singular hypotheses for statistical generalizations inductively inferred from evidence. We can never be certain of generalizations, since they are logically independent of their supporting evidence. A logical probability, in contrast, is entailed by the evidence, and is hence known. For the same reason he introduces, as we have seen, logical information to specify prior probabilities for contingent hypotheses. This insures that for a sample that is uniformly *B* we can never be justifiably certain that the next individual will be *B*.

The basis for this skepticism has already been discussed and rejected in Section 2.2, and these criticisms need not be repeated. It is sufficient to note that when the skeptic maintains that it is only "probable" that the sun will rise tomorrow or that this pencil will "probably" drop if released he is inventing a new sense of the term 'probable' very different from that we ordinarily use. The term 'probable', like 'uncertain', is used to make a contrast. We say 'It will probably rain tomorrow' as a way of qualifying our assertion and contrasting it to cases where we make a categorical, unqualified assertion. Such a qualification is out of place when we say 'The sun will probably rise tomorrow'; here the categorical 'The sun will rise' or 'I know the sun will rise' would be used to indicate no reasonable doubt is entertained. Similarly, we do in fact accept generalizations into our background knowledge and accord them the status of "laws" in the manner discussed in Section 1.3. To say that these too are only "probable" is to fail to make an essential contrast between those generalizations accorded the status of a law and generalizations that are tentative hypotheses still in the process of being tested.

Nonskeptical versions of probabilism attempt to account for these obvious features by formulating rules of acceptance that rely on assigned logical probabilities.[27] Intuitively, we seem in fact to accept hypotheses when they pass a certain "threshold" of probability relative to the evidence before us. At some stage we require, according to these versions, no higher a degree of confirmation for a hypothesis, and eventually accept it as true. The problem becomes then one of determining the specific probability that can serve as the numerical threshold for justified acceptance. There are several ways of fixing such a probability level, each with its special difficulties.

Let us concede for the purposes of argument what the previous section has denied and suppose that a method can be devised for assigning numerical values to the degree of confirmation of a hypothesis h relative to evidence. One possible criterion for rational acceptance of h would require that h be "not unreasonable," and set a probability of ½ or greater as the standard. This is the level that seems to be set by Roderick Chisholm. We must distinguish, Chisholm says, between the decision to accept h and the decision whether or not to act upon it. The decision whether to act upon a hypothesis requires consideration of the utility attending the consequences of such an action and consideration also whether we should inquire further. In contrast, the decision to accept is made only on the basis of whether we have adequate evidence.

> The question whether to *accept* a certain hypothesis—whether to believe it—is thus easier to answer than the question of whether to *act upon* it. In deciding whether to accept it, we need not consider the "utility" or "moral gain" that would result from acting upon it. And we need not consider whether we ought to make further inquiry and investigation.[28]

Given this separation of acceptance from action, Chisholm regards himself free to state a very weak condition for acceptance. The condition is that we not have adequate evidence for the hypothesis' contradictory, for "it is only when we have adequate evidence for the contradictory of a proposition that it is unreasonable for us to accept the proposition."[29] Assuming the probability or degree of confirmation of -h relative to evidence e must be greater than ½ for e to be "adequate evidence" against h, Chisholm's standard requires for the rational acceptance of h that h relative to e have a degree of confirmation of ½ or greater.[30] We may not be willing to act on the basis of an h with a probability as low as ½ and we may wish to subject it to further testing, but we should nevertheless accept it as true.

It is clear that Chisholm means by 'accept' what we would term 'not reject' or perhaps 'provisionally accept'. As a criterion for terminal acceptance into the status of background knowledge his is obviously too weak. Recall from the previous section that according to Hintikka's method we assign to all uniform generalizations of the form 'All *A*s are *B*' the prior logical probability of ½, a rational number which is gradually increased with the number of instances that confirm it. By Chisholm's criterion, then, *every* such uniform generalization that has not been disconfirmed should be accepted, even though there is no positive supporting evidence. This is much too inclusive, even for provisional acceptance.

Attempts to set the probability threshold higher, however, also encounter difficulties. Shall we set it at .8, or at .95? Or is it to be .995 or .999? Any number seems to be arbitrarily selected. Moreover, any number we select runs afoul of what is known as the "lottery paradox." Let us set .999 as the acceptance threshold. Suppose then there are 1,000 tickets issued for a lottery, one each to 1,000 different individuals, and that there is a fair drawing for the winning ticket's number. Then the logical probability of the first individual a_1 not losing (or winning) is .001, and for losing the probability is .999. Let h_1 be the hypothesis that a_1 loses in the lottery. Since this is our threshold, we should accept h_1. Similar considerations would hold for the acceptance of $h_2, h_3, ..., h_{1000}$, each stating that one of the remaining individuals will not win. Each of these alternatives should also be accepted on the basis of passing the threshold. It follows that we must accept the conjunction h_1 & h_2 & . . . & h_{1000}, since we accept each of the conjuncts. But we know that $p(h_1$ & h_2 & . . . & $h_{1000})$ = 0, since at least one of the 1000 individuals will win. Hence, we are lead to accept as true a hypothesis whose logical probability is zero, and this is clearly absurd.[31]

An alternative to stipulating an arbitrary rational number is to define a criterion for rational acceptance relative to a disjunction of competing hypotheses h_1 v h_2 v . . . v h_n which purport to explain the same phenomenon, e.g. hypotheses stating alternative causes of a certain disease. Then a possible rule of acceptance would prescribe acceptance for that hypothesis h_i whose degree of confirmation relative to evidence *e*, or $c(h_i/e)$, is greater than that for any other alternative.[32] This rule does avoid the problem of fixing a threshold probability, since the probability leading to acceptance will vary with the alternative sets of hypotheses being considered. But there is another difficulty just as serious. Suppose that hypotheses h_1, h_2, and h_3 attributing viruses Y_1, Y_2, and Y_3 as causes of a disease are the alternative hypotheses under consideration. Suppose also that a degree of confirmation of .55 can somehow be assigned based on limited evidence to h_1, while h_2 and h_3 are assigned .54 and .53 respectively. Then by this acceptance rule the investigator should accept h_1. But clearly such acceptance may be unjustified if further testing could be expected to allow a more decisive ranking between the alternatives. Rather than accept at this preliminary stage, the more reasonable course would seem to be to delay a decision pending the acquisition of more conclusive evidence.

The acceptance rules considered so far have all been stated in terms of a relation between a hypothesis and supporting evidence. Philosophers of science have also formulated a number of supplementing criteria for deciding between competing hypotheses whose degrees of confirmation assigned by the alternative probabilist measures would be exactly the same. Such criteria have been stated in terms of the forms of the hypotheses themselves and have included their relative simplicity and explanatory power and the projectibility of their predicates.

Included in such criteria is also that of the relative informativeness of the hypotheses, with the more informative hypotheses selected over the less.[33] This introduction of information content is made by Popper when he introduces the criterion of "severity" of tests in deciding between alternative hypotheses as an alternative to sheer numbers of confirming instances. Information content in itself, however, seems to be irrelevant to justified acceptance when we are attempting to decide between alternative empirical generalizations, for normally competing hypotheses, e.g. whether virus Y_1 or Y_2 is the cause of disease Z, have the same information content. In contrast, at the level of theories we can sometimes distinguish between those theories that enable more precise predictions than others, and here information content can be relevant. What normally allows us to decide between types of functional correlations, including those at the theoretical level, however, is the development of more precise means of measurement, not the forms of these correlations themselves. As we saw in Section 3.2, it is progressive applications of the Functional Precision Rule that allow us to falsify theories previously supported by less precise measurements of its variables. The information content of a theory is, in fact, no greater than the degree of precision with which we are able to provide measurements of its variables. Further, we shall see below in Section 4.4 how increased information content is often not itself a desideratum in scientific inquiry. There are many circumstances in which investigators choose a lesser content because it can be more easily tested relative to available evidence.

The fundamental objection to all these alternative rules is their assumption that acceptance of a hypothesis is justified relative only to the hypothesis itself and its relationship to an existing body of evidence. Ignored completely is the role of the procedural rules discussed in Section 3.2, rules which because they are openended confront us with the problem of deciding the extent to which they are to be applied. Probabilism attempts to avoid this problem, first by transforming the inductive relation between premises and a defeasible conclusion into a deductive relation used for assigning probabilities, secondly by dismissing as irrelevant variation rules in favor of randomizing rules for which the sheer number of confirming instances is itself sufficient for raising logical probability, and finally by justifying acceptance in terms of these assigned probabilities.

The pragmatist alternative is to acknowledge the relevance of our purposes to the application of open-ended procedural rules requiring decisions for terminating the search for additional evidence. To determine exactly how they are relevant is the central problem of the next chapter.

Chapter 4

The Pragmatist Alternative

Pragmatism denies that acceptance of a proposition p can be justified solely in terms of a dyadic relation between p and a body of evidence from which p's probability can be logically derived. Instead, its alternative is to state a necessary condition for the acceptance of p in terms of the fulfillment of interests and purposes to which this acceptance is related. The formulation of this condition is now our principal task. In Section 4.1, I discuss some difficulties with Carnap's "Principle of Total Evidence" and give examples of how judging sufficiency of evidence is relevant to acceptance. In Section 4.2 a pragmatic condition for justified acceptance is formulated that requires the investigator to weigh the costs of obtaining further evidence against the cost incurred if the accepted proposition were to later prove mistaken. In Section 4.3 the contrast is noted between the acceptance of a proposition in the context of practical inquiry where a specific action is being entertained and acceptance in the context of theoretical inquiry where there are no specific applications. I argue that for theoretical inquiry also a pragmatic condition is necessary for justified acceptance. Here potential costs of error, which vary with the centrality of the science within which a specific hypothesis is formulated, include wasted research effort. The next section shows the relevance of information content of a proposition p to the costs of both obtaining evidence and adjustments to the falsification of p. In general, the higher the information content of p the more difficult and costly it is to obtain evidence on which to base its acceptance, and one way of protecting against falsification is to lower information content. Finally, I discuss some results of studies in cognitive psychology indicating that norms governing scientific inquiry are regularly violated by persons in everday situations. I interpret these results in a way consistent with the principles developed earlier in the chapter.

4.1 SUFFICIENCY OF EVIDENCE

We have seen how probabilism assigns probabilities to a hypothesis h on the basis of a logical relation between h and a body of evidence e, and then attempts to state rules for accepting *h* that employ these probabilities. Assumed in the assignment of probabilities is what is known as the "Principle of Total Evidence." As formulated by Carnap this is the assumption that the evidence used by a person X in assigning a probability to an *h* includes all the relevant information known to X, in Carnap's words, "his total knowledge of the results of his observations,"[1] all the evidence *e* which X actually possesses relevant to *h*'s degree of confirmation. There may be further evidence *e'* available to X beyond *e*, which he could acquire if he were to carry out a further search, but this cannot be considered in assigning probabilities, nor can it be considered in deciding whether or not to accept *h*. The Principle of Total Evidence thus requires, as Kyburg notes, that we should "use all the information we have, not in the sense that we should go on collecting information indefinitely."[2] Whether we should act upon *h* may depend on whether further evidence *e'* should be acquired. "Before we *act upon* any hypothesis," Chisholm says, "we should also consider whether *additional* inquiry or investigation is indicated. . . . If we plan a minor operation, one specialist may be enough; but if we plan a major operation, we should call in others."[3] But as we saw in Section 3.5, Chisholm in common with other cognitivists insists on separating the question of whether to accept *h* from the question whether to act upon it, and hence the problem whether further evidence is required is regarded by him as irrelevant for acceptance.

There is no need to repeat at length the criticisms in the previous section of this separation of acceptance from both action and the decision whether to acquire further evidence. This separation leads directly to the difficulties encountered in formulating rules of acceptance. As a result, probabilism can offer no justification for imposing a more stringent condition beyond Chisholm's weak rule permitting acceptance for what is not unreasonable. Suppose, for example, we adopt the method used by Hintikka outlined in Section 3.5 for assigning probabilities to universal generalizations. Initially a hypothesis such as 'All swans are white' has, as we saw, a logical probability of ½. If our evidence includes a positive instance of a single white swan, then this probability is slightly increased. Why not accept the hypothesis on the basis of this single confirming instance? Why require more confirming instances? In fact, probabilism can give no answers to these questions, since any probability threshold will be arbitrary. By requiring only that the total evidence for assigning a probability to a hypothesis be the actually possessed evidence probabilism fails to explain why additional evidence should ever be required.[4]

It is possible to formulate a version of the Principle of Total Evidence requiring not simply possessed, presently obtained evidence, but all the available evidence, the evidence that could be obtained if a search were to be continued.[5] This is not a principle that could be applied, however, since for virtually every scientific hypothesis the total evidence in this sense will be indefinitely large, and hence the search for it could never be terminated. For a uniform law-like generalization of the form 'All *A*s are *B*', for example, any sample, no matter how large, will be smaller than the total population of *A*s. It is obvious that often we require more than the evidence currently at hand prior to accepting a proposition. But it is just as obvious that at some stage we must terminate the search for additional evidence if acceptance is to be possible.

Acceptance is thus inseparable from the decision whether to seek out further evidence, since it includes the decision to terminate the search relative to the actions that are to be based on this acceptance. To seek further evidence on which to base generalizations is, as we saw in Section 3.2, to follow procedural rules that by their openended character fail to specify a cut-off point beyond which there is to be no further applications. By what criteria then do we terminate a search and decide presently possessed evidence is a justifiable basis for acceptance? Some examples of inquiry suggest an answer, and these we now consider.

Perceptual Identification

Examples illustrating the relevance of practical goals to acceptance and termination of inquiry are readily available in perceptual identification. Someone hands me a pencil and asks if it is mine. I say 'Yes' after only a glance, and put it in my pocket. It looks sufficiently like the one I have been using to warrant accepting the proposition that it is my pencil. But if a district attorney were to hand me a pistol used by another in a recent robbery and ask me if it were mine, though it may look like mine at first glance, I would carefully examine it, searching for tell-tale marks or scratches, before giving my answer. Obviously, the importance of what is at stake determines the difference in the care with which I examine the objects. If the pencil is not mine, virtually nothing has been lost because of the mistake. In contrast, a mistake in identifying the weapon may mean an innocent person will be punished.

For classifying an individual object as an instance of a kind an analogue of the procedural Ascriptive Variation Rule is used, with cost considerations relevant to how extensively the rule is to be applied. We saw in Section 1.3 how background knowledge can be of a form in which attributes are transferred to a general subject term as the result of accepting either uniform or statistical generalizations and then become used as criteria in the identification of objects. Thus, if generalizations 'All *A*s are B_1' or 'All *A*s are probably B_1', 'All *A*s are probably B_2', . . . , 'All *A*s are probably B_n' are accepted, $B_1, B_2, . . . , B_n$ become criteria for identifying an individual as an *A*; the possession of a certain indefinite proportion of these attributes becomes a necessary condition for being an A. The procedural rule for identification is then the following

Identification Rule: Prior to identifying an object as an instance of A, check to determine whether the object satisfies criterial attributes B_1, $B_2, \ldots, B_n$ to the extent feasible.

As for all procedural rules, the "to the extent feasible" provision is the point at which pragmatic considerations must be introduced. Consider, for example, a party of amateur botanists on a trip to identify the wild flowers of a certain region. They make such assertions as 'This is a flower of species Y' and 'This other is probably a Z' on the basis of a cursory inspection of such features as coloration, size, and shape. Contrast this now to what is accepted by a group collecting mushrooms for an evening meal who must distinguish between those edible and those poisonous. They would examine mushrooms for coloration, size, and shape, but would undoubtedly also look carefully at habitat and perhaps cut open some to inspect their interiors. Of course, background knowledge may lead to these extra precautions if it were to inform of two different species similar respect to coloration, size, and shape. But the principal reason for increasing the number of attributes examined prior to accepting an identification of an individual as a member of a certain species is that the extra effort is justified by the cost of a mistake.[6]

Trusting Witnesses

Just as obvious examples are provided by cases where we must decide whether to check on what is told us by others or to simply accept their reports unchecked. Someone tells me there are fish to be caught about one hundred yards away, and I go immediately to try my luck. But if I were told about fish in a distant lake ten miles away I would probably want to check with some independent source before making the long trip. A mistake here would involve much wasted effort. Similarly, we normally trust authorities about routine matters, as when a mechanic informs me of a problem with my car, and I order the repair. But a governmental committee deciding on the allocation of funds for an expensive repair of a bridge would probably call in several expert witnesses to diagnose the bridge's defects and the feasibility of repair. As before for perceptual identification, background knowledge in the form of information about the reliability of witnesses plays a role in determining how extensive a search for further evidence is justifiable. The testimony of an unreliable witness should obviously be checked on. But the principal factor in deciding whether to accept or to check further will be the potential costs of a mistake as weighed against the effort expended in conducting the check.

Medical Diagnosis

More complex examples illustrating the relevance of cost considerations to acceptance are presented by medical diagnosis. Weinstein and

Fineberg offer the example of a physician confronted with a patient complaining of frequent need to urinate and urinary tract irritation.[7] The physician suspects a bacterial infection in the patient's urinary tract, although there are no fever or chills. He considers taking a culture of the urine to test for bacterial growth, but the result of this will not be known for two days. He must decide now, however, whether to treat the patient with an antibiotic to which he may have an adverse reaction or wait for two days until the results of the culture test come in. The latter course of action could cause the patient's condition to worsen. To prescribe the antibiotic now, Weinstein and Fineberg say, is to accept the proposition that the patient has or probably has a urinary tract infection, a decision in which the cost of a mistaken diagnosis in terms of needlessly prescribing a potentially harmful drug is weighed against the cost of first obtaining more evidence and delaying treatment until the culture is in. Normally in such situations if the drug is prescribed, the culture is also taken. If the later results show the diagnosis to have been mistaken, the drug would be withdrawn from treatment.

It should be noted that the basic features of the problem confronting the physician are not altered if the proposition being accepted states a probability. Suppose that his background knowledge includes the statistical generalization that the probability of urinary infection for persons exhibiting the patient's symptoms is .75. Then by a direct inference the physician could infer that the probability of this patient having the infection is .75. It is this proposition that he accepts when he prescribes the drug. There is no need to say, as do the probabilists, that the physician has a reasonable degree of belief of .75 in the proposition. The physician simply accepts the objective individual probability as true, and acts in accordance with it.

Discussions in recent epistemology also provide examples illustrating the need to assess the feasibility of securing additional evidence. I summarize here one of the most widely discussed.

Harman's Letter

Gilbert Harman presents what is intended as a Gettier-type example of justified true belief without knowledge in which available but ignored evidence seems decisive in assessing a knowledge claim. We suppose there is a man Norman who goes to Rome but wants to deceive his friend Mary into thinking that he is staying in San Fransisco. In order to do so he writes Mary a letter postmarked from San Fransisco telling of his plans to stay there. The letter arrives but lies unopened and ignored on Mary's desk. Meanwhile, Mary on the basis of other reliable evidence forms the reasonable and true belief that Norman has gone to Rome.[8] Though Mary may correctly and justifiably believe that Norman is in Italy, Harman claims that she does not know that he is. The reason is that there is evidence available to her (the unopened letter) that would lead her to revise her belief if she were to obtain and make use of it (open and read it). Accepting a proposition as what one knows requires for Harman also accepting that there is no negative evidence that is available but unpossessed. It is this latter acceptance that Mary cannot justifiably make, and this failure leads us to withdraw any claim made on behalf of her knowing that Norman is in Italy.

Harman's solution of his own problem is defective in several ways. First, he distinguishes between Mary's reasonable belief in Norman's being in Rome from her accepting this proposition as known, assuming that the evaluative term 'rational' or 'justified' can be applied to belief in the way criticized above in Section 2.3. So far as 'rational' can be applied to Mary's belief, it is being applied to her acceptance of the proposition that is the content of the belief. Whatever reasons we have, then, for criticizing her acceptance of the proposition as known extend also to her belief in this proposition.[9] Secondly, Harman distinguishes between the acceptance of a proposition p and the acceptance of a second proposition p' that there is no negative available evidence against p, claiming that the former presupposes the latter. But from the standpoint of the person X faced with the decision of whether to accept p no such distinction exists. Whatever evidence supports p also necessarily supports p'. Finally, Harman maintains that it is the existence of unpossessed evidence not taken into account by Mary, the letter lying unopened on the desk, which defeats the claim to her knowing. But as William Lycan has pointed out, our reason for denying knowledge here is not the mere existence of unpossessed evidence. Almost invariably, as we have noted, there is available evidence that is unpossessed, and hence Harman's requirement would make knowledge virtually impossible. What defeats the knowledge claim, Lycan correctly argues, is the "ready accessibility" of the evidence, the fact that the letter lies conveniently on the top of the desk.[10] If the letter were buried under a pile of letters or even lying undelivered in the central post office, we would be less inclined to withdraw the knowledge claim. It must also be added that we would assess Mary's efforts towards obtaining such evidence by the importance to her of Norman's whereabouts. If this is of little interest to her, letting the letter lie unopened would seem to be perfectly justifiable, and the claim to knowledge would remain unchallenged.[11]

All of these examples are ones in which a person X must decide whether or not to accept a proposition p relative to possessed evidence e given the fact that there is additional available evidence e' that X could obtain with further effort. Relevant to this decision is the cost of obtaining e' as compared to the cost to X if p were to prove mistaken. But exactly how are such cost considerations relevant? To answer this question is to formulate a pragmatic condition for rational acceptance.

4.2 THE PRAGMATIC CONDITION FOR ACCEPTANCE

Before attempting to state this condition we must define some key terms. For an action, activity, or state of affairs A to have a *cost* for a person X we shall simply mean that X has an aversion towards A. For A to be *more costly* to X than some other A' is for X to have a stronger aversion towards A than towards A'. Similarly, for X to regard A as having a *benefit* is for X to want or desire to do A or have A brought about, and for A to have *more benefit* than A' for X is for X to prefer A to A'. In the context of practical deliberation an agent must typically weigh the costs of performing some action A against the benefit of some state of affairs B which is a consequence of A and an end to which A is a means. The costs of A include the time, resources, and energy that must be expended in its performance and other consequences B' to which X may have an aversion. The costs include also *opportunity costs,* costs incurred when we forego the opportunity to enjoy or secure some benefit. X's decision that he should do A is based on his preference to incur these costs rather than forego B's benefit.

By the *utility* to X of A is meant A's benefit to X and by A's *disutility* its costs. For A to have more utility for X than A' is thus for X to prefer A to A'. The philosophic tradition has interpreted the term 'utility' to stand for the psychological states of pleasure or happiness. But since such states are so difficult to predict and determine, even for ourselves, let alone for others, this interpretation makes it virtually impossible to apply the term in actual practice. We do know, however, what we and others want, and hence interpreting 'utility' and 'disutility' in terms of desires and aversions does make it possible to apply them. The philosophic tradition has also sought to distinguish between an agent X's *desire* for A and the *desirability* of A for X. But assessments of desirability for an individual X are made from the standpoint of some other person Y or the community of which X is a part, and either Y or the community imposes its own desires in making these evaluations.[12] The important distinction is between an individual's wants and preferences and the wants and preferences shared by members of a community and for which there is community consensus. This distinction is especially important in the context of scientific inquiry, where the costs or disutilities of evidence acquisition that are relevant in evaluating rationality of acceptance are principally social or moral costs, not prudential costs to the individual investigator considered in isolation.

If an individual or community can express preferences between actions or states of affairs $A_1, A_2, \ldots, A_n$ they can provide an ordinal ranking of their utility. Whether besides ranking $A_1, A_2, \ldots, A_n$ it is also possible to express *how much* one is preferred over another and hence provide cardinal measures of their respective utilities is a matter of some dispute.

Assuming quantitative measures of utilities are possible, with 1 assigned to the "best" of a number of actions or states, 0 to the "worst," and rational numbers to those intermediate, utilities can be combined with probabilities to calculate what is known as the *expected utility* of an action. Let us suppose than an action A, e.g. drilling for oil at a certain site, has two possible outcomes B_1 and B_2, e.g. discovering a large quantity whose utility measure is .9 or a moderate quantity of oil with utility of .5. Suppose also that the probability p_1 of outcome B_1 is .4, while the probability p_2 of B_2 is .8. Then the expected utility of A is the product of the probability p_1 and the utility u_1 of B_1 added to the product of the probability p_2 of B_2 and its utility u_2, or $(p_1 \times u_1) + (p_2 \times u_2)$. For our example the expected utility of drilling would thus be $(.4 \times .9) + (.8 \times .5) = .36 + .40 = .76$. More generally, for an action A with possible outcomes B_1, B_2, . . . , B_n whose probabilities of occurrence are respectively p_1, p_2, . . . ,p_n and whose utilities are u_1, u_2, . . . ,u_n the expected utility of A is $(p_1 \times u_1) + (p_2 \times u_2) + . . . + (p_n \times u_n)$.

Controlled situations where there are measurable monetary gains and losses provide the typical examples used for calculating expected utilities. Even here numerical measures are difficult. In the decision situations we face in daily life utility measures are impractical, even if in the rare cases where they might be technically possible. Instead, we rely on rough, intuitive judgments of our degrees of want or aversion towards consequences of our actions and rough estimates of the probabilities of these consequences coming about. I must decide today whether or not to bring my umbrella to work. In making this decision I must weigh the inconvenience of carrying it against the expected cost to me if it were to rain. This expected cost is some indefinite function of how hard it may rain, whether a drenching thunderstorm or light shower, to which I have differing degrees of aversion, and the likelihood of these events. It is where there is a low probability of a thunderstorm (based on a weatherman's forecast) or a high probability of a shower that the decision becomes difficult, for here the expected costs of not carrying the umbrella approach those of carrying it.

With these preliminaries aside, let us now attempt to determine how an agent's wants and aversions influence his decision to accept a proposition *p* as true and terminate the search for further evidence. The examples of the preceding section suggest that what influences such a decision is a comparison between the costs of continuing the search for evidence and the costs of the consequences of acting upon *p* if it were mistaken, costs to both X and possibly others who might be affected by the action. The higher the costs of a mistake the higher the costs that X and the community of which he is a part are willing to incur in acquiring further evidence. This suggests a pragmatic condition requiring that for X to be justified in accepting a proposition *p* relative to evidence *e* as true the cost of acquiring additional relevant evidence e' must be higher than the cost of acting on the basis of p that would be incurred if p were to later prove mistaken. As has been emphasized, background knowledge will play the role of determining what additional evidence is "relevant."

To this delimited domain of relevant evidence the condition just formulated is applied in the manner illustrated by the examples of the preceding section. For the perceptual identification of the pencil a glance is sufficient, while for the pistol of the robbery a careful inspection is required because of the higher cost of a mistake. We take the word of the local mechanic about our car while a governmental committee requires several independent expert witnesses to determine the bridge's defects. An error about the bridge could result in the large sums of money spent on repairs being wasted, while an error about the car brings only the inconvenience of returning it again to the same mechanic or perhaps turning to another. Similarly, the physician accepts the diagnosis of urinary infection without waiting for the outcome of the urine sample test because a misdiagnosis can be corrected two days later when the test results come in without significant harm to the patient. And finally, we regard Mary as not justified in accepting the proposition that Norman is in Italy because, even though it is true and supported by evidence, additional evidence in the form of the unopened letter is readily available and Norman's whereabouts is presumed to be important to her.

But while the pragmatic condition we have formulated may be able to account for these examples, it runs afoul of others. I accept the proposition that the ceiling above me is safe. It would be disastrous for me if I were wrong and it should collapse on top of me. It would take comparatively little effort for me to check on its safety, but I nevertheless regard myself as justified in accepting its safety, contrary to the pragmatic condition. Again, the tires on my car might be defective, and if they were I might be involved in a serious accident. But I accept the proposition that they are safe before driving out on to the highway for a short trip, even though it would cost comparatively little time and effort to have them checked at the local garage.[14] What such examples show is not that it is a simple comparison of costs that is employed in evaluating acceptance, but rather a comparison between a cost of acquiring evidence, which is usually quite certain to be incurred, and a cost of a mistake, which we estimate as having a varying degree of probability of occurring. It is not the *cost* of a mistake which is to be compared with that of acquiring additional evidence, but the *expected cost* of actions if there were to be a mistake as a function of the probability of the consequences of these actions occurring and our aversion towards them. It is because it is highly unlikely that the ceiling above me will collapse or my car's tires blow out on a short trip that the expected cost of these states of affairs is low. For this reason my acceptance of the propositions is justified.

Accordingly, we can reformulate our condition by simply substituting 'expected cost' for the occurrences of 'cost'. It now becomes the following

Pragmatic Condition: X is justified in accepting a proposition *p* relative to evidence *e* as true only if the expected cost of acquiring additional relevant evidence *e'* is higher than the expected cost of acting on the basis of *p* which would be incurred if *p* were to later prove mistaken.[15]

Where statistical generalizations for determining probabilities of outcomes and numerical measures of their utilities are both available we can interpret the expression 'expected cost' of the consequences of the actions as 'expected utility' and calculate it as the sum of products of probabilities and utilities. If, as is almost always the case, either numerical probabilities or utilities are lacking, rough estimates of expected costs must suffice. Thus, based on the frequency of ceilings collapsing I estimate the expected cost of staying in the room as negligible, disregard further available evidence, and justifiably accept the proposition about safety on which my staying is based.

To this improved version of the Pragmatic Condition cognitivists will immediately raise the following objection. In this version reference is made to the expected cost of the consequences of acting on the basis of *p* if *p* were to be mistaken. But it would seem that *p* itself must be used in calculating these expected costs, and hence we are already using the very same proposition whose acceptance is being justified.[16] Thus, the proposition I now accept is that the ceiling above me is probably safe. But this is what is used to determine that the expected cost of the ceiling collapsing on top of me is less than the cost of acquiring further evidence. I am thus using the proposition whose acceptance is being justified in order to determine whether or not this justification is warranted, and this is clearly circular. The circularity seems to show that there must be a prior acceptance based on purely epistemic considerations before pragmatic factors can be introduced. Consider also the physician diagnosing that the patient probably has a urinary infection and on this basis prescribing a drug. In determining the expected cost of a mistake, in this case prescribing a wrong drug to which the patient may be allergic, the physician would also be using the diagnosis whose acceptance is being justified. Again, the circularity shows, cognitivists will argue, that there must be some prior forms of acceptance for which the Pragmatic Condition is not necessary.

This objection represents a misunderstanding of the basis for determining expected costs. It is never the terminally accepted proposition that is itself used as the basis. It is rather the proposition as provisionally accepted in conjunction with background knowledge resulting from previous acts of acceptance. For example, we noted above that the physician may have available statistical generalizations stating that the probability of a patient with certain symptoms having a urinary infection is .75. It is this probability, along with perhaps the probability of patients having an allergic reaction to the drug he plans to administer, that allows him to calculate the expected cost of a mistake. By means of a direct inference the physician could infer that this particular patient has the urinary infection with a probability of .75. But as we saw in Section 3.3, this inference requires accepting the further premiss that this patient is similar in relevant respects to the subjects sampled in the survey establishing the generalization and deciding not to acquire further statistical data relevant to special attributes of the patient. If a singular probability proposition is accepted by the physician, then it is, in effect, the proposition that this patient is in fact similar to the subjects in the sample. It is to this proposition that the urine test whose results are delayed is relevant, for it furnishes additional information not known about the sampled subjects, and hence establishes an attribute that distinguishes the patient from what is known about the sample. If the singular probability is itself used to calculate expected costs of a mistake, it is only in provisionally accepted form pending this additional information.

This distinction is also clearly present for my acceptance of the ceiling's safety. What I accept is that the ceiling *is* safe, not that it is probably safe, with the basis for the acceptance my casual observation that the ceiling looks like a normal ceiling. It is this categorical proposition that a careful inspection of the ceiling would either confirm or falsify and to which the Pragmatic Condition is applied. This proposition is not that used in determining the expected costs of error referred to in stating this condition. Instead, for this determination we use background knowledge, including the proposition that ceilings in general almost never collapse, a proposition whose scope of reference is wider than the singular proposi-tion being presently accepted. If a singular probability about this ceiling were to be used in calculating costs, it would only be in a tentative form pending information about whether this ceiling is similar in relevant respects to those described in the background knowledge.

In general, let p be a singular proposition about an individual accepted by a person X by ignoring additional available evidence e', and let A be an action based on p whose consequence if p is mistaken is B. Let q be be a statistical generalization used in determining the expected cost of B. If p is a singular probability derived from q by means of a direct inference, then what X accepts is that the individual being referred to is alike in relevant respects to the members of the sample on which q is based, for it is this to which the ignored evidence e' will be relevant. If p is used to calculate expected costs, it is used only as provisionally accepted pending information about its derivability from q. If p is a categorical proposition, then it is distinct from q. In none of these cases, then, is the proposition as accepted by X used in determining expected costs of B.

The examples just given have been singular propositions, but it is obvious that this account can be extended to generalizations as well. Consider, for example, a wheat importer faced with the problem of assessing the quality of a given shipment of wheat by determining the proportion of grains in the shipment that are spoiled. Sampling of wheat is done from different areas of the ship's hold or at different intervals as it is being transferred to other containers. Let $p(B/A) = r$ be the proposition stating the probability that a grain of wheat is spoiled. The more extensive the sampling the less the risk that a given r will be later rejected as not describing the proportion of spoiled wheat. By the Pragmatic Condition how extensive the sampling required before accepting an r as the probability of spoilage will be determined by comparing the cost of increases of the sample to the expected cost of assigning to the shipment the wrong rating of quality. As for the singular propositions about infection and ceiling safety, background knowledge about the probability of assigning a wrong rating on the basis of such a sampling procedure will be used to assess the expected cost of a wrong rating, and the propositions forming this background will be, as before, distinct from that for which a decision about acceptance must be made. If $p(B/A) = r$ is used to calculate expected costs, it is only in a provisionally accepted form based on presently available evidence. There is no decision at this stage to terminate evidence search, and hence no terminal acceptance.

There is also a second objection that can be raised against the Pragmatic Condition so far as it implies that if the expected cost of additional evidence e' is less than that of a mistake then acceptance cannot be justified. Let us suppose than an investigator X considers accepting a proposition p relative to evidence e and that the additional e' can be subdivided into small increments, $e_1, e_2, \ldots, e_n$. This would be the situation if p were a generalization of the form 'All As are B' and the increments were individual As added to an existing sample. Let us suppose also that the cost of acquiring any individual increment e_1 (adding an individual to the sample) is minimal, but that the total cost of e' as the sum of increments does outweigh the cost of p's being mistaken. Then let t_0 be the initial occasion at which X considers p relative to existing evidence e. The cost at t_0 of adding e_1 is minimal, and hence X should not at this stage, according to the Pragmatic Condition, accept p relative to $e + e_1$, the sum of the existing evidence plus the first increment. But also at a subsequent occasion t_1 the cost to X of adding e_2 to the now existing evidence $e + e_1$ would be minimal, and hence acceptance cannot be justified at this second stage. These considerations would hold also at time t_2 where the cost of adding e_3 is again minimal, and indeed at every subsequent occasion up to t_{n-1} where e_n is to be added. At none of these subsequent occasions can acceptance of *p* be justified by the Pragmatic Condition. Yet by the assumption of our example X is justified in accepting *p* relative to the totality of evidence *e'* whose cost does outweigh that of a mistake. The Pragmatic Condition thus seems to evaluate acceptance of *p* as both rational and irrational.

The argument is, however, utterly fallacious, being analogous to that of a fat man claiming on successive occasions that eating any single piece of candy is not harmful to his health and then proceeding to eat the whole box. The term 'additional evidence' used in stating the Pragmatic Condition refers to the totality of evidence acquired between the occasion at which a proposition is initially considered or provisionally accepted and the occasion of terminal acceptance. It does not refer to successive increments of this evidence.[17] Just as we would criticize on utilitarian grounds the fat man for eating the box of candy, so we would criticize the investigator of our example who at occasion t_n would have acquired more evidence than reasonable relative to cost comparisons.

It must be stressed that while the Pragmatic Condition is a necessary condition for acceptance, no claim is being made here that it is in itself sufficient. Other purely epistemic conditions will undoubtedly also be necessary. One is that the inductive rules of Section 3.1 be complied with, though we shall see in the final section of this chapter how this condition can be challenged. It has been frequently pointed out in the philosophy of science that it is possible to have alternative hypotheses that are "indeterminate" with respect to existing evidence, that is, equally confirmed relative to it, and for which no further acquisition of evidence could be justified. In such cases we may have to apply such criteria as the relative simplicity of the forms of hypotheses or the projectibility of their predicates. Information content is also one of these additional epistemic criteria that is often invoked, but we shall see in Section 4 how this cannot be separated from the Pragmatic Condition just outlined. It should also be noted that this condition states a *comparison* between costs of a proposition *p* being mistaken and evidence acquisition. It does not state that acceptance is justified relative only to the consequences of acting on the basis of p, an alternative version of pragmatism that has often been advanced. This other version will be considered in the next chapter.

4.3 THEORETICAL INQUIRY

So far we have applied the Pragmatic Condition only to propositions used as bases for particular actions. The need for such a condition in order to explain our actual practice of acceptance, assent, and assertion is relatively obvious for the examples that have been discussed. But many have objected to the extension of this condition in order to justify the acceptance of hypotheses in the context of theoretical inquiry. The end of such inquiry, they argue, is truth for its own sake, not specific applications, and the potential applications are so numerous and diverse as to make any estimate of the cost of a mistake impossible.

That some scientific inquiry is conducted without specific applications in mind is undeniable. The physician in our example in Section 4.1 may have accepted the diagnosis of a patient as having an infection as a basis for prescribing the drug. But this diagnosis was based on a statistical generalization that 75% of patients exhibiting his symptoms also had the infection. The acceptance of this statistical generalization antedated the physician's specific application of it, and this acceptance was thus certainly not made in anticipation of the physician's diagnosis. Similarly, an engineer may accept the proposition that a certain metal is strong enough to withstand a given force and apply this in the construction of a bridge. There are specific costs that can be anticipated if the singular proposition about *this* metal is mistaken. But this proposition is based on background knowledge provided by chemistry stating that metals of that kind have a certain level of strength, and the prior acceptance by the community of chemists of the relevant functional correlation was made independently of any particular action and its potential costs. Both of these examples are of generalizations arrived at by "applied" science. The independence of acceptance from applications is even more obvious in the so-called "pure" theoretical sciences where the structures of galaxies, subatomic particles, living cells, and other phenomena are investigated. Here the basic motivation seems to be only the urge to unlock the mysteries of nature, and investigators with this curiosity seem to have only an incidental interest in later applications.

Moreover, let us suppose that a certain proposition p is accepted relative to several actions among which A_1 and A_2 are included. Then as Levi has pointed out, acceptance of p might be justified relative to A_2 but not to A_2 if the costs of a mistake differed for the two actions.[18] For example, let p be the proposition that a certain vaccine Z has no harmful side effects on mammals, a proposition inductively based on testing with a wide variety of mammals. Then p could be used as both a basis for an action A_1 of a physician inoculating a human patient with Z and for an action A_2 of a veterinarian inoculating a horse. Clearly the costs of p's being mistaken for the physician we would judge to be much greater than for the veterinarian. Thus, an extent of testing justified for accepting p relative to A_2 might not be justified relative to A_1 with its higher costs. But this leads us to conclude that acceptance of the same proposition could be both justified and unjustified.

What such examples show, however, is that consequences of specific actions cannot be used in estimating the costs of general hypotheses as the objects of scientific inquiry. But it is possible for the consequences of an indefinite range of actions to be anticipated in terminating experimental testing and accepting a hypothesis as true. This would surely be done in testing the side-effects of a vaccine. If the range of potential applications included use on humans, much more extensive testing would undoubtedly be required than if its use were restricted to domestic animals. For the hypotheses considered in "pure" research the range of potential applications is much less definite than for "applied." But from past experience we know that discoveries in physics and physical chemistry have led to the development of new materials for industrial applications and new forms of energy, while discoveries in biology and organic chemistry have lead to advances in medicine. The cost of a mistaken hypothesis includes, then, the opportunity cost of delaying or foregoing altogether these benefits. These costs cannot be calculated in terms of specific probabilities and utilities of outcomes. This does not prevent, however, their being compared with costs of evidence acquisition and used in decisions about the extent to which procedural rules are to be applied in experimental testing.

Provisional acceptance of a hypothesis as a candidate for testing provides clear and far less controversial examples of vaguely anticipated benefits determining acceptance. Background knowledge is relevant to determining whether a given hypothesis h is initially plausible as consistent with what has been previously accepted. But in addition the potential benefit gained from the successful confirmation of h must be weighed against the costs of testing, and even a hypothesis judged initially implausible might be subject to testing if these benefits were large and the costs of testing relatively low. This is apparently what Peirce means when he claims that cost considerations are the only "serious consideration" in provisional acceptance.

> Proposals for hypotheses inundate us in an overwhelming flood, while the process of verification to which each one must be subjected before it can count as at all an item, even of likely knowledge, is so very costly in time, energy, and money—and consequently in ideas which might have been had for that time, energy, and money, that Economy would override every other consideration even if there were any other serious considerations. In fact there are no others.[19]

Faced with limited resources society through its policy makers must decide which research proposals should be funded, e.g. whether an expensive particle accelerator is to be constructed or a program of biological research to be carried out, and obviously the potential benefits of this research is considered in making these decisions. The fact that these benefits cannot be precisely calculated does not prevent such decisions from being made. But then this lack of specific information should also not prevent decisions of terminal acceptance being made which require imprecise estimation of costs of mistakes, since these costs will include foregoing the benefits whose anticipation initiated testing.

Though for theoretical inquiry opportunity costs constitute one type of cost or error, there are also costs of a very different kind. Recall from Section 1.3 that background knowledge resulting from terminal acceptance is used in providing presuppositions of questions to which hypotheses are proposed as answers. It is also used to interpret observations, transfer meaning from predicates to subjects for subsequent identifications, and to provide assumptions used in deriving experimental consequences and explaining deviations of the observed from the predicted. In such cases the actions based upon accepted propositions are not designed to attain a specific purpose, as in practical inquiry, but instead are actions furthering future inquiry. As has been emphasized, though we term the result of such acceptance "knowledge," any proposition that has been terminally accepted and used in any of these ways may later prove to be mistaken. Such a mistake will often invalidate a program of research based on the assumption of the mistaken proposition, and hence result in a waste of the time, resources, and energy invested in this program unless an easy adjustment to the error can be made. To the opportunity costs of mistakes in theoretical inquiry, we can thus add the *wasted effort* cost of error in background assumptions.

The potential for this type of cost varies with what we can term the *centrality* of the hypothesis under consideration. By this is meant the extent to which, if accepted, the hypothesis will guide future inquiry for the science within which it is formulated and the extent to which this science furnishes assumptions used by others. For example, physics can be regarded as a more central science than chemistry, for it provides a framework of assumptions within which much of chemistry is conducted, while it proceeds relatively independently of any background knowledge provided by chemistry. In the same way chemistry is more central than biology, biology more central than physiology, physiology more central than behavioral psychology, and psychology more central than sociology. Within each science there are similar orderings of centrality, with some accepted propositions used as assumptions in the testing of others. Theories as complexes of general propositions occupy the most central positions in the sciences. As Lakatos has noted, for the scientific community to accept a theory is to commit some of its members to an entire program of research, with a series of new questions and methods for answering them following as consequences of the newly accepted theory.[20] Carrying out such a program requires substantial investments of resources, time, and energy, much of which would be wasted if the theory were to be later rejected. Hence, acceptance of a theory should occur only after the most thorough testing to reduce the likelihood of this waste.

In contrast, acceptance of propositions at the periphery of science should warrant a more casual inductive basis.

Two contrasting cases illustrate how centrality affects the extent of evidence acquisition. Consider a botanist describing a species of wild columbine as part of a project of classifying the wild flowers of a certain region. He or she would probably base this description on a small sample for which there has been minimal effort to vary attributes relevant to those predicated in the description. If the description were published, it would undoubtedly be readily accepted, with little effort made by others to check on its accuracy.

Contrast this now with a microbiologist describing the mechanisms by which substances are transported through a cell membrane. Before his or her description is published there would be extensive use of variation procedural rules and extensive checks to confirm its accuracy. After publication its experiments would be repeated by other investigators, and after only thorough independent testing would the description be accepted by the scientific community. This contrast may be partly due to the difficulty of observations at the molecular level and the increased risk of error. But it would be principally due to the relative centrality of the two descriptions, the fact that the membrane description after acceptance would become background knowledge used in an indefinite variety of future investigations, while the columbine description is at the periphery of science with little future use other than in the classification for which it was originally intended. The potential wasted effort cost is minimal, while that for the membrane description is significant. In this way the Pragmatic Condition is applicable to descriptions of theoretical science independently of any future practical applications.

The extent to which openended procedural rules are applied in the theoretical sciences is determined by two factors. One is society's willingness to invest the funds necessary to purchase equipment and provide support for those applying the rules in testing hypotheses. The extent of application is also regulated in a more important way by what we shall refer to as *limitation norms,* which determine the extent and thoroughness of evidence acquisition. These norms have evolved as an adjustment to the different cost considerations of a mistake and the consequent demands on evidence acquisition in these disciplines, and impose standards of care and thoroughness that are transmitted by laboratory and field training to successive generations of investigators. It is through following different limitation norms that investigators in botany require less extensive application of procedural rules than those in microbiology. This important feature of scientific activity is emphasized by what has been called "methodological pragmatism," a version of pragmatism to be evaluated in the final chapter.

We can conclude, then, that there are no grounds for exempting theoretical inquiry from the scope of the Pragmatic Condition. What must be recognized is only the distinctive way this condition is applied, a way that tends to be masked because of the nature of science as an institutionalized specialization and the sometimes indirect influence that social interests have on scientific practice. It is probably essential for the success of theoretical inquiry that individual investigators not be obsessed with concerns about the Pragmatic Condition in their decisions to accept or reject and that their primary motivation be curiosity and the urge to discover what they regard as the "truth for its own sake." Certainly it is essential that not all inquiry be directed by specific social goals, for history teaches that the greatest practical gains often result from discoveries made by those who *thought* they were engaged in disinterested inquiry. But in fact disciplines within science have different norms regulating the extent of application of procedural rules, and it is the differing requirements for evidence acquisition imposed by these norms that only the Pragmatic Condition can justify.

4.4 INFORMATION CONTENT

Among the cognitivist rules of acceptance discussed in Section 3.5 was one that justified acceptance relative to the "epistemic utility" of a proposition as a function of the proposition's information content. To apply such a rule is to regard informativeness as a desideratum to be maximized in order to make the proposition more vulnerable to falsification. In fact, however, information content is dependent on the same pragmatic considerations in terms of which acceptance is justified. To explain the nature of this dependency is the purpose of this section.

The information content of a proposition is a function of the range of alternatives indicated by the question to which it is an answer.[21] So-called "whether" questions such as 'Did it rain last night?' or 'Is a swan white?' have two alternative answers, 'Yes' and 'No', and hence a specific answer will convey relatively little information. A "what" or "which" question, in contrast, will present a wider range of alternatives, the number of them being dependent on the type of subject or predicate in the question and the context in which it is asked. For example, 'What color is a swan?' would probably be taken to indicate the alternatives 'white', 'yellow', 'brown', 'red', among others, from which the answer is to be selected, while 'Which color is the wall painted' would indicate specific shades such as 'egg-white', 'ivory', 'chalk white', or others as the alternatives. Hence, an answer to the latter question will convey more information than for the former. For measurable magnitudes such as 'width', 'length', 'velocity', 'weight' there is a similar dependence on subject and context. 'What is the length of this table?' in an everyday context may prompt an answer such as '3 feet, 6 inches', thus excluding such alternatives as '3 feet, 5 inches' and '3 feet, 7 inches', since accuracy to the nearest inch would be sufficient. But 'What is the length of this screw?' would require an answer with accuracy to the nearest $\frac{1}{16}$ of an inch and 'What is the length of this strand of DNA molecule?' asked in the context of microbiology may require an answer to the nearest fraction of a millimeter.

Probability propositions offer another example of a measurable magnitude that can be specified with more or less exactness, depending on the question being answered. For 'How likely is it that it will rain tomorrow?' we would answer in everyday situations by the expressions 'very likely', 'likely', 'may', or 'unlikely'. We could also reply by saying, as do the weather forecasters, that there is a 10 percent chance, as contrasted to a 20, 30, 40, percent chance, thereby conveying by the answer more information than previously. For statistical generalizations inductively inferred from proportions in samples or frequency in trials there will be differences in information content that depend on the interval of error. For a given generalization $p(B/A) = r \pm \delta$, the larger the interval δ the lower the information content. As noted in Section 3.3, this interval is a function of the size of the sample or number of trials. Hence, raising the information content requires increasing the amount of evidence upon which the generalization is based and the cost of its acquisition.

This relationship between cost and information content holds generally for every proposition. To say only 'Object Z is white' as contrasted with predicating 'yellow', 'brown', etc. is to assert what can be confirmed by a quick glance. In contrast, to convey more information by saying 'Z is ivory' would probably require more careful scrutiny for confirmation, and perhaps even comparison with a color chart, with a consequent greater expenditure of time and energy.

For measurable magnitudes these differences in cost can be significant. The description 'This man is tall' can easily be confirmed, while 'He is 6 feet 2 inches' could be checked only with a tape measure. More accurate measurement requires special instruments and perhaps a repetition of a measurement in order to calculate a mean value, and both increase the costs of evidence acquisition. Thus, the cost of measuring the length of a strand of DNA molecule to the nearest fraction of a millimeter would be appreciable, while that for measuring the diameter of a proton with the precision required in physics still greater. Every functional correlation has variables ranging over the nondenumerably infinite real numbers. The information content of such a correlation will depend on the interval of possible error for a given measuring procedure. Let $m_1(A)$ be a specific measurement m_1 performed relative to some magnitude A, e.g. length, weight, temporal interval, or velocity. A given measurement will be of the form $m_i(A) = x_i \pm \epsilon$, with x_i a specific rational number that is the outcome of m_i and ϵ the estimated interval of error relative to the measuring procedure that is followed. As the precision of measurements increases and the interval ϵ is reduced, the finite number of alternative rational number values excluded by a given measured value $x_i \pm \epsilon$ increases, and with this increase comes an increase in the information content of the functional correlation being tested. Again, such increases of information content are attended by higher costs of constructing instruments and increasing the number of measurements.

Physical theories as complexes of functional correlations with wide scope of reference exhibit the same relationship between precision of measurement and informativeness. Hence, as precision increases, a theory at a later stage of development may convey more information than it did at an earlier stage. This increase of information is often followed by the falsification of a theory. Thus, the introduction of the telescope and Brahe's measurements of the positions of the planets enabled the later falsification of Ptolemy's theory of the solar system and its replacement by Copernicus' theory. Similarly, Newton's theory of gravitation initially conveyed a level of information that was a function of the accuracy of the measurements of the positions of the planets made by Brahe. Subsequent increases in the accuracy of measurements of the motion of the planet Mercury led to its falsification and replacement by Einstein's theory.

It is to such examples that Levi seems to be appealing when he notes that increasing information content brings with it the risk of error, and that we therefore forego this increase to avoid the risk.[22] In fact, there are a variety of ways in which the information content of a proposition is limited in order to enable acceptance of it as true, and each of them involves pragmatic considerations of the same general nature that limit evidence acquisition.

The relevance of these considerations is exhibited in the different strategies available for adjusting to the falsification of a generalization. Suppose our hypothesis is a universal ascriptive generalization such as 'All swans are white' and that we use the direct inference,

$$\frac{\forall x(Ax \supset Bx)}{Ba_i}$$

to predict that a given individual a_i which is an A is also B. In Section 3.1 we discussed two adjustments that can be made to this falsification. One is to restrict the scope of the subject term A by identifying some other attribute C which the As that are B share in common. Another is accomplished by converting the uniform generalization 'All As are B' into a statistical generalization stating that an A is probably a B. Both retain B as the predicate of the generalization. But there is another possible adjustment that can be made that decreases information content by retaining the original subject while expanding the sentence's predicate to include the attribute D of the a_1 which is not B. The predicate then becomes the disjunction $B \vee D$, and the sentence is of the form $\forall x[Ax \supset (Bx \vee Dx)]$ ('All swans are either white or black'). A similar adjustment can be made for falsified causal generalizations by replacing the description of the effect by one more indefinite.

If making the predicate more indefinite adjusts to falsification, then clearly we can anticipate this in our initial choice of predicate. For every generalization of the form $\forall x(Ax \supset Bx)$, whether ascriptive or causal, it is usually possible to replace the predicate B by another B', which is equivalent to $B \& D$ in which D is a further specification of B, and in this way increase information content. Thus, instead of 'All swans are white' we might choose 'All swans are ivory white' and instead of 'Administering drug Y will cure patient Z' formulate 'Drug Y will cure Z within two days'. Such replacements increase the risk of falsification for the same reason that decreasing information content adjusts to falsification.

Why is a less informative predicate B chosen over a more informative B'? The answer is that increasing information content brings with it, as we have seen, an increased cost of obtaining the evidence required to test it, and the benefit of precision may not be sufficient to offset this cost. Propositions are stated as answers to questions, and there is usually some specific use to which these answers are to be put. Thus, a zoologist often wants to know the attributes of a given species in order to distinguish it from others in the process of constructing a classification and to identify in the future individual members. The precision of the predicate B will be only such as to fulfill these purposes; any beyond this could not be justified in view of the extra costs it would impose. Similarly, the question 'What is the cause of disease B?' might be asked in the context of medicine in order to develop a cure for the disease. The effect B will then be specified in its answer only to the extent necessary to attain this end.[23] Scientists are like fishermen who must decide on the size of the holes of their nets. A net with large holes can be dragged easily through the water, but many smaller fish will escape. As the size of the holes decrease the difficulty of dragging increases, though with this also comes an increase in catch. The limiting extreme is material with no holes. It would not be a net, and would be impossible to drag through the water, no matter what the effort. Just as fishermen must weigh the value of the fish to be caught against the difficulty of dragging, so scientists must weigh the purposes of inquiry against the difficulties and costs attending more informative hypotheses.

Physics seems to pose an exception to this process of reducing information content for pragmatic reasons, for in the process of developing ever more accurate methods of measuring its variable magnitudes with instruments of greater and greater cost physicists seem to be striving for unlimited information content. It is his use of physics as a paradigm that undoubtedly leads Popper to conclude that the sciences in general have as their aim the maximization of information.[24] Advocates of cognitivism generally will also argue that the special character of the theories of physics discloses science's goal of giving increasingly more accurate descriptions of the underlying nature of the physical universe. For practical purposes we may accept approximations for the reasons that have been given earlier in this section, but for the theoretical purposes of accurately describing physical structures these should be regarded as but intermediate stages to be surpassed as more precise measurements become possible.

In the previous section, we have already encountered this same theoretical-practical distinction in another guise; it should be rejected for essentially the same reasons as given there. Botany and zoology are parts of the theoretical sciences, and their descriptions often have no practical applications. Yet the accuracy of such descriptions, as we have seen, is limited by costs of evidence acquisition as compared with the opportunity costs of not fulfilling the purposes of the description. There are similar limitations in descriptions of physics. The rest mass of a proton is currently recorded to be 1.6725×10^{-24} grams. Even if it were technically possible to carry out this measurement to the next several decimal places, in the absence of any use for more precision the costs required for it would probably not be incurred. The search for more precision in measurements raising the information content of physical theories can be accounted for by their centrality in science, the fact that when accepted they provide background knowledge for other sciences in a way that is unique. It is this rather than the intrinsic worth of informativeness that justifies society's incurring the sometimes substantial costs of progressive increases in precision of measurement and the attendant risks of falsification.

4.5   VIOLATIONS OF NORMS OF INQUIRY

In recent years cognitive psychology has investigated the strategies employed by persons with no special scientific training in identifying objects and inferring conclusions.[25] They have found that there are significant divergences between the identification and inferential strategies used in everyday situations and those regarded as acceptable in scientific inquiry, that norms accepted by the scientific community as governing inferences are systematically violated. These violations take three principal forms: (1) identifying an object without surveying its different attributes; (2) hasty generalization from a small sample to a conclusion; and (3) continuing to accept a proposition despite falsifying evidence. (1) and (2) are violations of what we can term *procedural norms.* These are specific interpretations of the "to the extent feasible" provisions of openended procedural rules governing the acquisition of additional evidence. Procedural norms are guidelines that have evolved within the special sciences, which place constraints on what is "feasible" in the thoroughness and extent of evidence acquisition. As we shall presently see, violations (1) and (2) illustrate how the Pragmatic Condition has been applied in the evolution of procedural norms. Violation (3), in contrast, illustrate features of adjustment to falsification discussed in the preceding section.

Prototype Identification

In Section 4.1 we noted how criterial attributes for identifying objects come to be employed as the results of prior acceptance of both universal and statistical generalizations. Where statistical generalizations provide background knowledge a given attribute B_i may not be a necessary condition for an object being of a certain kind. There is a high probability that a bird will fly, and flying would be used as a criterial attribute identifying birds. It is not a necessary condition, since there are birds that do not fly, e.g. ostriches and penguins. Other attributes, e.g. having two legs, may be necessary, but are not sufficient, since there will be other organisms having two legs that are not birds. In identifying an object as an A we use, then, a cluster of attributes $B_1, B_2, \ldots, B_n$ of which typically some are not necessary and no one of which is sufficient. The Identification Rule of Section 4.1 requires that the number of attributes in this cluster be increased to the extent feasible. Included within potentially criterial attributes will be those relatively difficult to confirm, as the mating habits of a species of bird will be relatively more difficult to determine than its shape and coloration. Mistakes in identification often arise from not expending the time and energy required to check whether one of these attributes applies.

Applying the Identification Rule requires examining an object prior to identification with respect to a certain number of separate attributes. Experimental studies with subjects asked to categorize objects indicate that in normal situations this is rarely done.[26] Instead, subjects tend to select a prototype instance from their everyday experience, form a representational schema of this prototype, and then identify an object by comparing it to this prototype schema. The general shape and size of the prototype are the salient features of the schema to which an object is usually matched.[27] Thus, subjects may choose a robin as their prototype of a bird and identify individuals as those to which the term 'bird' applies by their degree of similarity to this prototype with its characteristic shape and size. For subjects using such an identification procedure a crow is likely to be identified as a bird, while an ostrich or hummingbird would be much less likely, since the shapes and sizes of the latter diverge significantly from the prototype. The likelihood of error is thus increased the more a particular object diverges from the prototype with respect to the salient features being used. Such errors would tend to be corrected by employing an extensive cluster of criterial attributes in accordance with the Identification Rule.

While the identification procedure used in everyday situations is more liable to lead to error than that used in scientific practice, it represents no violation of the Identification Rule, and can even be justified by it. It can be regarded instead as the limiting case where a few attributes—the salient features of the prototype schema—are used in identification. To "check" whether or not the object has these attributes is not to carefully examine or perform a measurement, but to match it against the schema. The justification for using this procedure is that for the familiar macroscopic objects of our environment it is not very likely to result in misidentifications, since most objects of the relevant kind will be similar to the prototype being employed. There are many more robin-like birds in our normal environment—crows, warblers, sparrows — than there are ostriches and hummingbirds. Further, the cost of a mistake is minimal, since relatively little is at stake if a misidentification were to occur. The extra effort and energy required to carry out the identification procedure of a scientist constructing a classification system would thus not be warranted by any gains that could be reasonably anticipated.

Hasty Generalization

A second deviation from norms regulating inquiry in the sciences is related to the use of inductive inferences. Elementary logic texts commonly list as one of the informal fallacies of reasoning the "fallacy of hasty generalization," the fallacy of inferring a generalization from a limited number and variety of instances. Studies indicate that we regularly commit such a "fallacy" in our everyday lives.[28] For example, in order to draw a conclusion regarding the popularity of a given course among students at a college, persons are liable to sample only one or two students rather than an extensive number of those who have taken the course. Similarly, in order to assess the risk of a heart attack among the middle-aged there is a general tendency to use as an evidential basis the incidence of heart attacks among those with whom we are acquainted, a gross violation of the norms for amount and variation of evidence that would regulate the acceptance of a statistical generalization in medical research.

Again, though these are violations of norms governing scientific inference, there are no violations of ascriptive variation or randomizing procedural rules, since a sample of one individual is but the minimal limiting case satisfying these rules. Further, the departures from norms for sampling regulating the social sciences can be justified if either using a more casual procedure will not result in inferring a conclusion appreciably different from that obtained by a more extensive application of procedural rules or the cost of a mistake is minimal. Harman also notes how the benefit of "clutter avoidance" is typically a reason for terminating inquiry quickly. During inquiry we must keep track of the reasons and evidence for a proposition, as a jury must keep in mind all the conflicting evidence in the process of reaching a verdict. But once the proposition is accepted (the verdict reached), this record keeping can cease and the mind freed to pursue other areas of inquiry.[29]

Such pragmatic factors are recognized by Nisbett and Ross, who note that the inferential strategies of daily life cost relatively little to apply. In contrast, what logic texts regard as the "normatively appropriate" strategies for inferring conclusions

> are extremely time consuming and expensive. It may be clear what must be done if one wishes a correct answer to such problems, but sometimes it may be even clearer that the correct solution is not worth the effort. This gives rise to more important questions of normativeness which are not fundamentally empirical in nature: How much effort, for what kinds of problems, should be expended to obtain a correct solution.[30]

What they regard as the "correct" solution to a problem is that accepted by scientists employing an appropriate procedural rule. But we have seen how within the sciences there are significant variations in the requirements for evidence acquisition in peripheral sciences such as botany and zoology as contrasted to more central sciences such as physics and microbiology. And since procedural rules are open-ended, it is always possible, though perhaps not practically feasible, to impose more stringent requirements beyond those regulating any of the sciences. In this sense there is no absolute standard of what is "correct" with which to contrast the conclusions reached outside the context of scientific inquiry. The only standard with which to evaluate differences in extent of justifiable evidence search is that provided by the Pragmatic Condition.

With the exception of this qualification, however, Nisbett and Ross confirm the applicability of the Pragmatic Condition in explaining why commonly used procedures diverge from the norms regulating scientific inquiry. There is, in fact, no fallacy of hasty generalization relative to all the purposes to which inductive conclusions can be put. Hasty generalization is listed as a fallacy only because the epistemological tradition represented by logic textbooks has mistakenly sought a general justification of scientific norms over the informal heuristic strategies used in everyday life.

Belief Preservation

A final aspect of everyday practice in which there is an apparent violation of normative standards is the tendency of persons to retain beliefs in propositions in the face of falsifying evidence. The sources for this aspect are also the studies of cognitive psychologists of the kind cited by Nisbett and Ross. Once having accepted a proposition, they note, studies show that most people are loathe to give up their belief in it, and will change their belief only by the "brute force of massive amounts of probative, disconfirming data."[31] Such behavior is not restricted to situations of ordinary life. Philosophers of science have cited many historical examples of the community of scientists retaining theories in the face of what is prima facie falsifying evidence, choosing instead to either ignore this evidence, reinterpret it by rejecting an assumption used in describing it, or explain it away by introducing an ad hoc hypothesis. Thus, observed deviations of the motion of the planet Mercury from what was predicted from Newton's gravitational theory were initially explained away by postulating the existence of an unseen planet named "Vulcan" whose gravitational influence could explain the deviations on the basis of the theory. Newton's theory continued to be accepted until eventually replaced by Einstein's theory, which successfully explained the anomaly without the ad hoc hypothesis.

Does such behavior constitute a violation of normative rules? This is a question not easily answered. As has been emphasized, to accept a proposition is to commit oneself to a course of action with possible disadvantageous consequences if the proposition proves to be mistaken. In everyday life the costs of a mistake may be quite minimal, not great enough to justify initiating and carrying out tests of some new proposition p' that must replace the proposition p that has been falsified. Hence, in the absence of a suitable replacement the belief in p tends to persevere. Further, adjustments to falsification of a uniform generalization can be made, as we noted in the previous section, either by restricting its scope, converting it to one of statistical form, or making its predicate more indefinite. These adjustments will often have little effect on actions taken on the basis of the generalizations, and realizing this we often continue to accept them as true beyond what is warranted by the evidence. Without beliefs as a basis action would be paralyzed. It will often prove advantageous to retain a belief thrown into question in order to avoid such paralysis, especially if it can be easily modified without serious harm.

We have noted how in theoretical inquiry acceptance results in background knowledge guiding actions taken in subsequent inquiry. This subsequent inquiry takes the form of formulating questions, selecting viable alternative answers for initial consideration, and providing the assumptions used in testing hypotheses. In this way an accepted theory typically provides the framework for a series of research programs; to reject one without providing a more adequate replacement would thus lead to the suspension of these activities. It is because the research programs can often be expected to generate useful results even if the theory on which they are based proves false that the community of scientists tends to act conservatively towards its theories.

In their attempt to account for the tendency of subjects to persist in beliefs in apparently "irrational" ways, Nisbett and Ross note that "the perseverance tendencies of subjects . . . were so extreme as to force consideration of the possibility that the traditional scientific standards may not apply." The behavior may be evaluated as inappropriate "from the standpoint of rationality in the inferential contexts studied," they suggest, but appropriate relative to the "pursuit of important, higher order epistemic goals."[32] The considerations just raised indicate that these goals are pragmatic. In practice we seem to require for the rejection of a proposition p that the estimated cost of p's being mistaken outweighs for us the cost of applying inductive rules and procedures in replacing p by some other proposition p'. Even if p happens to be falsified by evidence, then, we could justify its retention if rejecting it were to fail to satisfy this condition. Persistence would be justified if the cost of p's being mistaken were estimated to be minimal and actions based on p had useful consequences which would be foregone if p were abandoned and a replacement either unavailable or difficult to establish.

But though human behavior seems to indicate that this cost condition is applied, is this a justifiable practice and can this behavior be evaluated as "rational?" Certainly in well defined contexts it can directly conflict with inductive rules in a way that if licensed would endorse Feyerabend's irrationalist claim that in inquiry "anything goes." Suppose our hypothesis is of the form 'All As are B' and that we find an individual a_i which is an A but not B. Then to persist in the belief in the hypothesis would clearly constitute a rejection of the General Rule of Induction prescribing the projection of an observed pattern on unobserved instances. In such a case failure to reject and adjust for falsification must be evaluated as irrational.

But the examples of apparently "irrational" behavior cited by cognitive psychologists and of rule violations in science by historians are seldom of this well defined nature. The subjects of the psychologists' experiments all know that in everyday situations what is called "evidence," e.g. the testimony of others, even the results of observation, may be mistaken. Often to persevere in a belief is simply to discount what past experience has proved to be sometimes unreliable. The retention of scientific theories exhibits similar features. Suppose that from a theory T plus assumptions $A_1, A_2, \ldots, A_n$ is derived an empirical consequence C which investigators decide is inconsistent with a report C' interpreting what they observe. Then they can consistently refuse to reject T if either their interpretation C' can be replaced by another, one of the assumptions $A_1, A_2, \ldots, A_n$ rejected, or they can introduce an ad hoc hypothesis explaining why C' rather than C was observed. Each of these strategies has been vindicated at one time or other in the history of science as preserving a theory later recognized as one that at that time should not have been rejected. Given the complex interplay between background assumptions that may be false and the prediction and description of observable consequences there is never a test of a theory, which if ignored, would constitute a clearcut violation of an inductive rule. In this sense it is not the case that "anything goes." Instead, there is a tendency to construct elaborate defenses around a theory, all consistent with the normative rules governing inquiry, and all designed to retain the benefits of continuing to pursue the research programs guided by the theory under attack. Like the stubbornness exhibited by belief perseverance in daily life, that in science is often justifiable.

The Pragmatic Condition is the central part of the theory of rational acceptance developed in this work. Having formulated this condition and shown some of its applications, I want to now compare and contrast this theory with versions of pragmatism developed in recent philosophy.

Chapter 5

Varieties of Pragmatism

Like most philosophical "isms," the label 'pragmatism' does not stand for a theory stating clearly defined theses. Nevertheless, it is possible to characterize the classical pragmatism of Peirce, James, and Dewey as making at least two general claims. The first is that scientific inquiry is an extension of the processes by which all organisms have adapted to their environment. As a consequence, certain basic features of the primitive interpretation of natural events combining anticipation of future events with actions to secure benefits and avoid harm (cf. Section 1.1) are also present in the interpretation of the complex descriptions formulated within the natural and social sciences. The second claim seems to be related to the first in some vaguely understood way. It is the negative one that the truth of a proposition does not consist in its correspondence with some independent fact or state of affairs in nature. Each of the early pragmatists offered a positive alternative to the correspondence theory of truth. For Peirce a true proposition is one that would be accepted in the long run by the community of inquirers if inquiry were to be indefinitely continued. For Dewey truth is said to consist in "warranted assertibility," while James is associated with the view that the truth of a proposition is determined by whether actions based on it have beneficial consequences. Both the first thesis and the negative second one are, I think, correct, but the positive alternatives to the correspondence theory offered by classical pragmatism require restatement. In the first two sections of this final chapter I review some of the reasons pragmatists have had for developing these alternatives and some of the principal difficulties they encounter. Of special interest is the alternative that defines rational acceptance of a proposition in terms of its usefulness, the view labelled here "consequentialist pragmatism." A version of this view and a comparison between it and the pragmatic theory of rational acceptance developed in the previous chapters is the topic of Section 5.2. In Section 5.3 a more viable form of this alternative is developed. In the final section I briefly indicate how a pragmatist criterion for rational acceptance can be extended to the evaluation of materialism as a metaphysical theory.

5.1 TRUTH AND ACCEPTANCE

In Section 1.4 we noted Peirce's insistence on the separation of theoretical inquiry from practical considerations and his ideal of science as the pursuit of truth freed from the "dross of subjectivity." Despite this apparent advocacy of cognitivism, what Peirce calls his "pragmatic maxim" provides the necessary basis for introducing purposes as "subjective" factors in assessments of rationality. His maxim is to "consider what effects that might conceivably have practical bearings we conceive the object of our conception to have. Then, our conception of these effects is the whole of our conception of the object."[1] Applied to science this has the effect of requiring operational definitions for scientific terms, definitions that specify observable outcomes when experimental tests are performed. Applied to philosophy, as Peirce makes clear, the effect of the maxim is to purge from metaphysics as meaningless those of its terms that fail to meet its standards.[2]

It is this latter application and a specific consequence which he draws from it that is indispensable to the development of pragmatism. An "incognizable reality," Peirce says, a reality or "world" independent of our conception of it and to which propositions can be said to "correspond" if true, is meaningless by the pragmatic maxim, for it has no effects with "practical bearing." His reasoning seems to be that if such a "reality" is thought-independent we could never compare our propositions to it to see if they correspond. Since we lack an external perspective to make comparisons, to postulate it will make no practical difference in our actual determinations of truth or falsity.

Peirce's alternative is to define the truth of a proposition in terms of its acceptance relative to available evidence, but at the same time maintain his principle of "contrite fallibilism" that any given proposition accepted on one occasion as true may later prove to be rejected as false. Hence, truth is not what is accepted, asserted, or assented to by an individual on a given occasion, but what would finally be accepted (asserted, assented to) by the community of investigators if inquiry were to be indefinitely continued. This famous passage summarizes his view.

> All the followers of science are fully persuaded that the processes of investigation, if only pushed far enough, will give one certain solution to each question to which they can be applied. . . .
> The opinion which is fated to be ultimately agreed to by all who investigate, is what we mean by the truth, and the object represented in this opinion is the real. That is the way I would explain reality. . . . reality is independent, not necessarily of thought in general, but only of what you or I or any finite number of men may think about it; and that, on the other hand, though the object of the final opinion depends on what that opinion is, yet what that opinion is does not depend on what you or I or any man thinks.[4]

Peirce's equation of truth with ultimate acceptance is open to several objections. There are countless inconsequential singular sentences such as 'The paper in front of DSC in his study was white at 2 P.M. on April 16, 1987' was accepted by me as true on the date described. I am confident that it is destined to never be challenged in the whole history of the human race. It is the "one certain solution" to the question of the paper's color at that time and place. But though accepted by me and never corrected in all of posterity, it seems quite possible for the sentence to be false, for lighting conditions to have been abnormal, for me to have suffered a malfunctioning of visual receptors, etc. Such final, unchallenged acceptance is not confined to trivial singular sentences. With the exception of such fundamental questions as 'What are the ultimate constituents of matter?' and 'What is the structure of the universe?', most questions posed in the sciences are eventually answered. Many answers are revised, but there are also many, especially those at the periphery of the sciences, that are retained, and we can be confident that they will never be challenged any more than will be my assertion about the color of the paper before me. Yet though accepted and "fated to be ultimately agreed to by all who investigate," they are based on a limited amount of evidence. There is no assurance that a more exhaustive survey of evidence, even though it will never be undertaken, would not lead to the falsification of a given answer and its replacement by another. To this it may be replied that Peirce did not intend to equate truth with what simply will be accepted in the long run, but instead with what what would be accepted if any ideally exhaustive search for evidence were conducted. But as we saw in Section 4.1, no ideal can be applied to evidence acquisition: there will always be unpossessed evidence that could be acquired, no matter how exhaustive the search; acceptance is always a decision to concede a certain level of incompleteness.

Finally, Peirce's theory seems inconsistent with his own starting point. His objection to postulating an "incognizable reality" to which propositions correspond if true is based on his view that such a conception violates his pragmatic maxim by having no conceivable practical effects. But this objection seems just as applicable to the conception of what is fated to be accepted in the long run. For us in the present such a theory is of no more practical use in determining whether a proposition is true or false than is the correspondence theory. Two principles seem alone essential to Peirce's view of truth. The first is the Fallibility Principle noted in Section 2.2 that the fact that a given proposition p is accepted as true at a given time never constitutes a guarantee that p will not be later rejected as false. The second, what we can refer to as the "Non-Distinction Principle," is that the distinction between our acceptance of *p* and the truth of *p* at the occasion at which *p* is accepted or at which the sentence expressing *p* is asserted or assented to is one that we are never in a position to make.[5] Both principles seem assumed by his theory, with the second principle a direct consequence of the pragmatic maxim. But his theory is itself not required by the principles and, indeed, offers no advantages and considerable disadvantages over and above what they themselves state.

A more recent theory called the "redundancy theory" in effect restates the Non-Distinction Principle, while avoiding the difficulties confronting Peirce. Advocates of this theory claim that to ascribe truth to a sentence is but to assert or assent to the sentence itself. No further information is conveyed by "'The cat is on the mat" is true' than would be conveyed by simply asserting or assenting to 'The cat is on the mat'. In opposition to the claim of the correspondence theory that to ascribe truth is to assert a correspondence to a language-independent state of affairs, for the redundancy theory truth ascription is redundant.[6] As for Peirce's "incognizable reality," language-independent states of affairs have for their advocates no role to play in truth ascriptions; to postulate them adds nothing with "practical bearings."

To be defensible the redundancy theory cannot be interpreted as also claiming that assent is itself sufficient for truth. Someone may point to a certain location and signal to me by means of an undulating motion of his hands that a snake is nearby. I recognize his intention and assent to his gesture as an iconic representation. But this would not be equivalent to ascribing truth to the gesture. The term 'true' only applies to conventional signs, and requires recognition that linguistic rules have been complied with, while the undulating motion is presumably a nonconventional iconic sign. The requirement to comply with social conventions independently of the whim of this or that individual is mistakenly confused by the correspondence theory with a requirement to conform to independent states of affairs.[7] Nor, of course, is to accept the proposition p expressed by a sentence as true or to perform the public speech acts of assent or assertion to deny that *p* may not be rejected as false on some future occasion. The Fallibility Principle requires that we always concede this possibility. The redundancy theory should be interpreted as claiming only that the distinction between ascribing truth and accepting, assenting to, or asserting a sentence as a conventional sign is one, which since from our perspective can never be made, is meaningless.

Interpreted in the light of the Fallibility and Non-Distinction Principles the redundancy theory presents an entirely plausible application of Peirce's pragmatic maxim to the conception of truth without the difficulties introduced by referring to what is "fated to be ultimately agreed to by all who investigate." Unfortunately for the history of pragmatism this theory has often been confused with another stating that a sentence is true if and only if it is rational to accept it as true or that it is one which we are in Dewey's words "warranted" in asserting.[8] This truth as warranted assertibility thesis is obviously false. A person may be perfectly justified in asserting or assenting to a sentence such as 'All swans are white' at one time t_1 relative to the available evidence, but later reject it as false at a later time t_2 on the basis of more complete evidence. The fact that the sentence is justifiably asserted at t_1 surely should not require that we admit at t_2 that it was true then. Alternatively, 'All swans are white' could be justifiably asserted at t_1 and justifiably denied at t_2 without its expressing a proposition that was first true and then later false. Yet this is precisely what the warranted assertibility thesis requires.

Putnam has attempted to revise this theory by claiming that truth is not warranted assertibility (or "rational acceptability," as he prefers to term it) as such, but instead warranted assertibility under "epistemically ideal conditions."[9] Presumably he means that it would not be possible for a sentence to be both justifiably accepted and then justifiably rejected if on the two occasions a completely exhaustive survey of all the available evidence were to be made, if all possible precautions against error were taken, since epistemically ideal conditions are by definition for Putnam those that guarantee convergence on what is accepted as true. But this kind of revision is open to objections similar to those just raised against Peirce's appeal to acceptance in the long run. There never is, nor can there ever be in principle, an ideally complete survey of evidence or an exhaustive number of steps taken to prevent error. In practice we apply the Pragmatic Condition to determine how extensive precautions are to be taken as weighed against the cost of a mistake, and for this kind of comparison an ideal of the kind invoked by Putnam has no application.

Therefore, we must reject the identification of truth with warranted assertibility. This leaves us with only the redundancy theory's claim that to ascribe truth to a sentence is just to accept, assert, or assent to it. It follows as a consequence of this claim, however, that the only fruitful question to ask is whether acceptance (assertion, assent) is justified on a given occasion. The question of whether sentences correspond to what is language-independent is meaningless, since we have no means of making the comparison required to answer it. But we can determine whether it is rational to accept a given sentence as expressing a true proposition on a given occasion. To make this determination is not to ascribe truth, as we have seen, and in this sense truth is not rational acceptability. But the determination is all that we can exercise self-control over and is our responsibility as our only means of avoiding irrational and impulsive acceptance. There is a close analogy to action. For a person to determine whether he ought to perform an action A is not for him to decide to do A; in this sense to make the normative judgment is not to make the decision. But to make the normative judgment is necessary to avoid deciding impulsively and our only means of exercising self-control over the action.

A pragmatist epistemology is characterized by the questions it chooses to ask, taking as its central goal the formulation of criteria for evaluating acts of acceptance. This is in contrast to the project of classical episte- mology that, as we have seen in Section 2.1, attempts to provide condi- tions for "knowledge" as a relation between a knower X interpreting a sentence and an independent state of affairs. One of these conditions is that the interpreted sentence corresponds to the state of affairs it purports to represent. The remaining conditions are then formulated in such a way as to guarantee that X's belief in the proposition expressed by the sentence is arrived at in such a way as to guarantee that the correspon- dence relation holds. Reliabilism is the most consistent attempt to for- mulate these conditions. Cognitivism also shares the assumption of this classical epistemology so far as it holds that it is only the form of a proposition and its logical relations to supporting evidence that can insure the justified belief necessary for the knowledge relation. We saw in Section 3.5 that the result is either skepticism or the setting of arbitrary "thresholds" of acceptance. Both are avoided if we abandon the assump- tions that lead to them and realize that acceptance is a decision made by persons either as individuals or collectively in groups, and like all deci- sions this has practical and moral consequences. Since these conse- quences are objects of desire or aversion, these attitudes can now be regarded as having relevance to conditions for rational acceptance in a way impossible when the problem is regarded as formulating conditions for knowledge. It is in this way that Peirce's maxim applied in defense of the redundancy theory can be regarded as providing the foundation for the pragmatic theory defended in this work.

Just how difficult it is to avoid the assumptions of the classical frame- work is shown by an interpretation that is readily given to the formulation of the Pragmatic Condition in Section 4.2. There the expected costs of acquiring evidence are compared to costs of acting on the basis of a proposition p if it were "to later prove mistaken." For p to be mistaken is within the classical framework for it to fail to correspond to an independent state of affairs, and if so, we would have assumed such a correspondence relation in formulating the condition for p's acceptance. But by the redundancy theory for p to be false is simply for p to be rejected as false, and it is in terms of such rejection that the phrase 'to later prove mistaken' should be interpreted. It can be argued that there will be many cases in which p's error will lead to costs, and p will never be recognized as false by any agents. But this is again to dogmatically reintroduce the distinction that any pragmatic theory of truth contests. Certainly the distinction is of no importance to present inquirers attempt- ing to decide whether or not to accept p.

The label 'pragmatism' is often associated through the writings of James and Dewey with another philosophical "ism" called *instrumental- ism*. This is the view that scientific theories are only devices for explaining and predicting observable phenomena and that a theory evaluated as true is simply one that is successful in performing this function. Instrumentalism also holds that theoretical terms such as 'electron', 'force field', and 'quark' do not refer to entities in nature, but rather stand for convenient fictions that are useful for heuristic purposes as ways of interpreting this theory in terms of analogues of everyday experience. Instrumentalism is contrasted with *realism*, the view that physical theories do describe entities and structures in nature, that a true theory is one that corresponds to independent states of affairs, and that theoretical terms do have existent referents.

It might be thought that to use Peirce's maxim to endorse the redundancy theory is automatically to commit oneself to instrumentalism. But this is not the case. Instrumentalism, just as much as realism, violates the maxim by assuming an ability to compare our theories with an "incognizable reality." To claim that these theories do not correspond to independent states of affairs and that their terms lack referents is to assume the same ability to compare theories with "reality" as is assumed by realism. In this respect it is a metaphysical doctrine of exactly the kind that Peirce's maxim is designed to avoid. A pragmatist epistemology can therefore ignore the instrumentalism-realism issue in order to concentrate on the more tractable problem of assessing the role of purposes in evaluating the rationality of acts of acceptance.

5.2 THE TRUE AS THE USEFUL

The difference between what is true and what is rationally acceptable just discussed is of importance in assessing the most popular versions of pragmatism. Through the writings of James, the doctrine is identified with the view that a true proposition is one that, if used as a basis for action, will have beneficial consequences, or that "the true is the useful." The extent to which James himself held this view is a topic of debate. Certainly he held it for metaphysical propositions for reasons we shall return to in the final section. Whether he also held this view for the descriptive propositions of everyday life and science is far less clear.[10] But apart from this problem of historical attribution, the view is of intrinsic interest, though more for its failings and what they reveal than its merits.

These failings were noted early in this century by Moore and Russell[11] who pointed out that there is in fact no reliable correlation between the truth of a proposition and the benefit accrued from acting on it. A person X may believe that a manufacturer of cameras will be successful with a new product being introduced into the market and on this basis invest in the company's stock. In fact, the new product proves to be a failure. Nevertheless, the price of the stock soars to new heights as the result of a take-over bid by a large corporation, and X reaps a huge profit. His belief proved false, but yet was very useful to him. Conversely, X's belief may have proved to be true: the new product was successful. Yet because of a downturn in the stock market there was a fall in stock price, and he suffered a huge loss. His true belief lead him to disaster. Often accepting what later proves to be true can be beneficial, and an action with beneficial consequences is often based on a proposition later recognized to have been true. But the correlation is not invariable, contrary to what is required by the "true as useful" theory.

The theory becomes more plausible, however, when restated as a theory of rational acceptance rather than truth. In this form it claims that a person X is rational in accepting a proposition *p* as true if and only if actions performed by X on the basis of *p* have beneficial consequences for X or if they fulfill X's purposes. As we have seen, it is possible for *p* to be rationally acceptable though later rejected as false, and hence Moore and Russell's counterexamples do not necessarily apply to the revised version. Though *p* may be true and have harmful consequences, it can be argued, it must not have been rational to have accepted *p* if this harm were to have occurred. And if a benefit were to have been a consequence, it follows that it must have been rational to have accepted *p*, even if *p* were to have been later rejected as false.

But even in this revised form the theory remains defective. To evaluate acceptance as rational is to assess responsibility for it, and such an assessment would seem unwarranted if the harmful or beneficial consequences were those that the person X could not have reasonably foreseen. If the harm or benefit were brought about by an unusual chain of circumstances or some random event, then we would not hold X at fault. Thus, the investor in camera stock may be regarded as justified in accepting that the new product will be popular if he has good reason to believe he will profit from investing in the stock. The fact that the stock falls because of a totally unforeseeable market collapse would not be grounds for withdrawing the justification.

A version of pragmatism that accounts for this feature of justified acceptance has been advanced in recent philosophy. It evaluates acceptance in terms of the expected benefits or costs of the consequences of acting on the basis of the proposition, in terms of whether these consequences fulfill or frustrate purposes. We shall label this version *consequentialist pragmatism*.[12] The condition it applies in evaluating acceptance is the following

Consequentialist Condition: A person X is justified in accepting a proposition *p* if and only if X expects that the consequences of acting on the basis of *p* will fulfill his purposes.

A weaker modified form of this condition is used by Braithwaite to select among alternate hypotheses. If for two hypotheses h_1 and h_2 the expected utility of acting on the basis of h_1 is greater than for acting on the basis of h_2, then for Braithwaite it is rational to select h_1 over h_2.[13] Expected utilities are calculated by combining probabilities of outcomes with their utilities in the manner outlined in Section 4.2.

What is the role of evidence in deciding on rational acceptance? The Consequentialist Condition justifies ignoring evidence altogether and even accepting what is inconsistent with it. Jack Meiland gives the example of a woman who suspects her husband of being unfaithful on the basis of evidence such as lipstick on his collar, blonde hairs on his jacket, etc. She wants to preserve her marriage and realizes that accepting that her husband is unfaithful would destroy the marriage by leading her to be indifferent and cool. She therefore decides not to accept this, despite the evidence to the contrary.[14] By the Consequentialist Condition the wife is justified in ignoring this evidence and accepting a proposition inconsistent with it. The sole justification consists in her expectation that believing in her husband's infidelity would have harmful consequences, and this can override purely epistemic criteria in the form of possessed evidence.

This conclusion seems most implausible, however, and is reached by trading on the ambiguity of the term 'reason'. Certainly we can cite a reason *why* the wife continues to believe in her husband's fidelity, namely her desire to preserve her marriage. Here 'reason' is used in the sense of a motivating cause of the state of belief. But, as Heil notes, this does not constitute a normative reason *for* accepting the proposition resulting in this belief.[15] It would surely seem irrational to accept the fidelity proposition in the face of the conflicting evidence, though we would certainly understand her belief state, that is, be able to explain it and assign it a reason in terms of a motivating cause. At least in such a case, then, the Consequentialist Condition produces an evaluation that is plausible only because of a tendency to confuse justification with explanation.

Where a proposition is supported by evidence the Consequentialist Condition can be more reasonably applied, but in ways that seem to pose the problem of circularity raised in Section 4.2. Consider again our camera stock investor deciding that a product will be popular and justifying this acceptance pragmatically on the basis of an expectation of future profit. Let e be the evidence he has for the proposition p that the product will be popular, e.g. early favorable ratings of the product, his knowledge of a technological innovation that it introduces, etc. On what basis will the investor now expect that he will make a profit? Obviously, it is the proposition p itself: he expects to make the profit because the new product will be popular. The same evidence e which supports p, then, will provide the rational support for the expected benefit. Suppose that p were a statistical proposition, e.g. that the probability of the product becoming popular is .7. Then in applying the methods of decision procedure to calculate the expected utility of investing this probability would be combined with a numerical measure of utility of the profit. Now it seems circular to use the proposition p both in estimating the expected benefit or utility of acting on the basis of p and in justifying the acceptance of p by the Consequentialist Condition by employing this same expected benefit. What is being justified would then be used in the justification. Moreover, it seems inconsistent to claim, as advocates of this form of pragmatism must, that evidence e supporting p is irrelevant to justifying p's acceptance when e provides the evidential basis for the prediction of an outcome that is used in the justification.

In Section 4.2 we avoided a similar circularity problem by distinguishing between the use of p on the basis of possessed evidence e to anticipate the cost of a mistake and the acceptance of p as a decision to not seek additional evidence e'. It is the same proposition which in conjunction with background knowledge is used to estimate the cost of a mistake and whose acceptance is justified by the Pragmatic Condition. But since acceptance involves a decision to ignore e' and the estimate of cost is made relative only to e and background knowledge, there is no circularity in stating the Pragmatic Condition. The situation is different for the Consequentialist Condition where the distinction between e and e' is irrelevant. Nevertheless, here also we can distinguish between using p in conjunction with background knowledge in order to estimate an expected benefit and deciding to accept p. The investor, for example, could use background knowledge about the relative frequency of success of investments in other companies like the particular camera producer he is considering along with his estimate of the new product's popularity in order to estimate benefits. To use the proposition about future popularity to estimate benefits is not necessarily to accept it as true; at this stage acceptance of the proposition is only provisional, merely for the purposes of making a tentative prediction. In contrast, the Consequentialist Condition is used to justify his terminal acceptance of the proposition, and hence there is no circularity.

While the circularity problem can be avoided in this way, another cannot. I have emphasized that much of theoretical inquiry has, at least initially, no practical applications, serving as the basis for no actions other than those promoting future inquiry. Certainly within this inquiry propositions are accepted as true, and such acceptance is regarded in most instances as justified. Yet the Consequentialist Condition cannot be applied to such cases, and its fulfillment is thus not even necessary for justified acceptance. It might be argued that we can at least anticipate a certain range of benefits if a proposition of theoretical science were true and we were able to find technological applications. But how can these possibly be relevant to the acceptance of the proposition? The fact that a hypothesis *h* if true would have substantial benefits would seem no more relevant to whether it should be accepted as true than the fact that if true it could lead to great harm, as in the case of a discovery of chemistry leading to the development of a poisonous gas used in warfare. Even in areas of applied science where there are more specific applications, resultant benefits and costs seem irrelevant to justifying acceptance. Suppose we have two competing hypotheses h_1 and h_2 about the cause of a certain type of cancer. The benefits to be expected from both of them would be the same, namely curing the disease for many patients. But then does it follow that acceptance of both is equally justifiable? Obviously not.

Why has the Consequentialist Condition failed where the Pragmatic Condition succeeded? One obvious reason is that the Consequentialist Condition is far too strong, since it is stated as a sufficient as well as necessary for acceptance. This has the effect of making evidence irrelevant to acceptance. But there is another less obvious reason. Acceptance is intimately related to action; to accept a proposition *p* as true is to act on the basis of *p*, either in advancing some specific purpose or in continuing inquiry that eventually advances more long-range purposes. Granted this, it is nevertheless mistaken to confuse the justification of the acceptance of *p* with the justification of actions performed on the basis of *p*. We justify or criticize actions on the basis of whether or not they fulfill our purposes by means of practical inferences in which descriptive premises accepted as true occur. But while these purposes are relevant to the justification of this acceptance, the two types of justification are clearly distinct.[16] The Pragmatic Condition avoids any such confusion between them in its comparison between costs of a mistake and costs of further evidence, a comparison independent of the question whether specific actions ought to be performed. Suppose a person X is deciding whether or not to perform action *A* on the basis of *p*. The conclusion that he ought to do *A* is based on the acceptance of *p*, as we saw in Section 1.2. But by the Pragmatic Condition the justification of *p*'s acceptance is not based on *A*'s justification, but instead in part on X's expectation of the cost of performing *A* if *p* were to prove mistaken as compared to the cost of further evidence acquisition. It is quite possible for X to decide he should accept *p* and then decide he should not do *A*. Though the costs of making a mistake may be minimal or further evidence search costly, the benefit may not warrant *A*'s performance. Not much lost, but then not much gained either. In contrast, for consequentialist pragmatism if *p* is accepted, *A* should be performed, since acceptance is justified solely in terms of *A*'s consequences.

So far as it has advanced the Consequentialist Condition, then, pragmatism has well deserved the criticisms levelled against it. The more qualified pragmatism defended in this work, however, is invulnerable to these same criticisms and remains a viable alternative to the cognitivism which has dominated recent philosophy.

5.3　THE EVOLUTION OF LIMITATION NORMS

Another recent version of pragmatism avoids the principal difficulties of the consequentialist pragmatism that we have been considering. This version states that we are justified in accepting a proposition p if and only if p's acceptance is in accordance with justified rules. A justified rule is in turn said to be one which when used to derive propositions that are acted upon by agents has consequences which fulfill their purposes. We have then the following

> *Rule Consequentialist Condition*: Let p be a proposition accepted by an agent X on the basis of rule R. Then X is justified in accepting p if and only if R is a rule which if followed will generally yield propositions which when used as a basis for actions fulfill the purposes of X and the community of which he (she) is a part.

We shall term this version *rule consequentialist pragmatism* as distinguished from the direct consequentialist pragmatism of the preceding section.[17]

Notice that in formulating this condition there is no mention of X's expectation that the rule he is following will prove beneficial when propositions derived by means of it are used as bases for actions. The rule is one governing procedures of inquiry within a society, and its members will tend to share the general expectation that by following the rule they will be successful. But this expectation itself seems to be irrelevant to whether or not the rule is justified. The members of a primitive tribe may accept the pronouncements of their medicine man about the coming of the spring planting and rainy seasons, using these pronouncements as the basis for planting their crops and fully expecting success. But if in fact the medicine man repeatedly makes mistaken predictions, we would criticize the rule being followed and their acceptance of the pronouncements as irrational. It is success in practice alone that serves as the standard for evaluating a rule, not expected success.

Can we ever be confident that a given rule is justifiable? A rule can be mistakenly established within a society, as for the primitive tribe of our example. But normally, evolutionary development tends to eliminate rules that lead to failure, and the very fact that a rule guiding inquiry is presently in use is evidence that it has survived this elimination process. Social and environmental conditions change, and a rule that was successful in one set of conditions may fail in another. But these changes are normally gradual and involve only relatively minor modification of rules. In the absence of any reason for modification the reasonable policy is conservatism and following rules that have survived long periods of trial applications.

The Rule Consequentialist Condition seems to give a plausible justification for the rules characteristic of modern science over the methods of oracle consultation, astrology, omen reading, etc. of earlier stages of human development. Their success in application accounts for the survival of scientific methods into the present. We use these methods in the present, confident that future acts of acceptance in accordance with them will provide the basis for actions that will also further our interests. It is in this way, it can be argued, that we justify these acts of acceptance in terms of rules surviving the elimination of those unsuccessful.

Difficulties arise, however, when we attempt to be more explicit about what we are referring to by the term 'rule'. From the first two sections of Chapter 3 we may recall the distinction between inductive rules used to infer generalizations from reports of observations and procedural or methodological rules prescribing precautions to be taken against possible error. Attempts to provide a pragmatic justification of the General Rule of Induction (cf. Section 3.2) encounter the same circularity problem as do other attempts to justify induction. Induction is justified, it has been argued, because it has proved successful in the past as a means of inferring propositions on which to base our actions. This past success can be anticipated to continue into the future, and for this reason we are justified in employing the General Rule of Induction in the present to project from observations to generalizations from which empirical consequences can be predicted. But of course to project from past success to future success is to use the very same rule that is being justified, and hence the justification is circular. The General Rule of Induction must be recognized as incapable of justification, as providing a standard for rational inquiry, but not itself capable of being evaluated in terms of some other standard.

A pragmatic justification also seems out of place when applied to procedural rules for reducing potential error. These rules seem instead to be formulated on a priori grounds by conceiving of the possible ways that a false generalization could be inferred from true premises by means of inductive rules and then anticipating ways of minimizing such defeat. Thus, we reason that an ascriptive generalization of the form $\forall x(Ax \supset Bx)$ could be mistaken as inferred from a sample of As that are B if the members of the sample shared some attribute C. In such a case the conclusion warranted by the evidence would then be $\forall x(Ax \ \& \ Cx \supset Bx)$, and it is quite possible that in the future an individual of kind A which is not C would lack the attribute B. The Ascriptive Variation Rule of Section 3.2 prescribes that we take measures to avoid this error by varying the attributes of the As that are relevant to their being a B. The rule is formulated by conceiving of a specific kind of precaution that can be taken to reduce the chances of error. Using such a rule may in façt allow us to derive generalizations that when used as bases for actions enable us to fulfill our wants. But such pragmatic considerations seem irrelevant to the formulation of the rule itself.

The situation is quite different when we consider norms that evolve prescribing the extent to which a given procedural rule should be applied. Recall that these rules are openended, that it is always possible to vary another attribute or causal factor or increase the precision of a measurement. The central argument of the previous chapter was that the Pragmatic Condition is the basis we have for evaluating the appropriate extent of application. But investigators do not typically make such evaluations on a case-by-case basis. Instead, norms regulating the extent of application of procedural rules, what in Section 4.3 we termed "limitation norms," evolve within the different scientific disciplines. It is these norms which investigators conform to, usually unaware of the background of costs, previous mistakes, or attempts to prevent their reoccurrence that lead to their development. The fact that the Pragmatic Condition was applied in the past in the formation of a norm makes it unnecessary to apply it to the testing of a specific hypothesis in the present. Much of the illusion of the disinterested "objectivity" of science stems from investigators being unaware of the evolutionary history of the norms guiding their present inquiry. The standards imposed by these norms are inculcated through the laboratory training of science's novitiates, a training that tends to make habitual their later application. This transmission from one generation to another thus tends to obscure their pragmatic origins from those in the present.

Examples of norms regulating the extent of application of procedural rules are provided by statistical inferences in the various special sciences. Recall from Section 4.4 how the interval of possible error for a statistical generalization is a function of the size of the sample from which it is inferred, decreasing as the sample size increases. A given interval represents a "significance" level within a given field of study, a level setting a standard for the extent of sampling required in order for a conclusion to be evaluated as "significant," as providing an interval of error for which there can be useful applications. This level will vary with the contexts and applications characteristic of this field. That for a survey of voter preferences to be used by political candidates in deciding which issues to emphasize will normally be lower than for a series of tests designed to show the probability of a trait appearing for interbreeding within a race of mammals. These norms setting minimum sizes of samples from which a statistical generalization is inferred will vary with the costs of mistakes as compared to costs of selecting additional members of the sample. The higher the cost of a mistake relative to evidence acquisition the smaller will be the interval setting the significance level. Such norms evolve on the basis of a past history of weighing costs and adjusting to the consequences of specific actions based on accepted generalizations. They then become codified, transmitted through schooling, and accepted as standards by successive generations of investigators.

These considerations all lead to the rejection of rule consequentialist pragmatism. It is not inductive or procedural rules to which pragmatic considerations are relevant. As we have just seen, they are relevant instead only to limitation norms specifying the extent of application of openended procedural rules for selecting evidence. The norms have in turn evolved by applying the Pragmatic Condition formulated in Section 4.2. This Pragmatic Condition thus formulates the *only* pragmatic consideration relevant to the evaluation of the acceptance of a proposition as rational or irrational. This evaluation can be given directly by the Pragmatic Condition itself. It is more common in the special sciences, however, for this evaluation to be made in the way just described relative to accepted norms, thus by-passing the often complex weighing of costs which the Pragmatic Condition would require for each particular act of acceptance. But the formation of these norms consisted of a series of past applications of the Pragmatic Condition, and it is in terms of such applications that the norms can themselves be evaluated.

It should be obvious that the range of propositions to which Pragmatic Condition is applicable is much more restricted than for James's version of consequentialist pragmatism. The Pragmatic Condition can be applied only to empirical propositions, those whose acceptance is based on observational evidence. But James intended his "true as useful" doctrine to apply principally to metaphysical propositions such as 'The mental is distinct from the physical', 'Man has free will', or 'God exists'. We turn now to consider in a very cursory way the problem of determining whether pragmatic criteria of a different sort can be applied to them.

5.4 PRAGMATISM AND METAPHYSICS

James's views on metaphysics are well known. Since metaphysical propositions are not empirical, their truth cannot be decided on the basis of their success in explaining and predicting. Instead, James contends that it must be decided on the purely pragmatic grounds of whether believing in them would be advantageous to the believer. In two famous essays[18] he argues that believing in the propositions that men have freedom of choice and that an eternal supernatural being exists would have favorable effects on the lives of those holding the beliefs, and that it is therefore rational for us to accept them as true. The reason for the Pragmatic Condition being inapplicable to metaphysical propositions should be obvious. No effort is expended in acquiring evidence relative to them. Indeed, metaphysical conclusions come very easily, often in an armchair, perhaps even while lying in a drifting boat; for certain types of people speculating about them is one of the chief pleasures of life. Since there are virtually no costs attending the reaching of these conclusions, there are no comparisons possible between these costs and the cost of a mistake. Without the requirement to weigh costs we seem forced now to appeal to the Consequentialist Condition and to conclude that we are justified in accepting a metaphysical proposition solely on the basis of whether it will fulfill our purposes. This would now be exactly the conclusion that James reached.

But is it one we should accept? We have already criticized consequentialist pragmatism for failing to distinguish between justifying acceptance of a proposition and justifying actions based on it. The fact that metaphysical propositions are nonempirical seems to leave unaffected the need to maintain this distinction. Why should their non-empirical character grant them an exemption? If our purposes are relevant to our acceptance or rejection of metaphysical propositions, then it would seem they are relevant in a different way than advocated by James's consequentialism. But what could this other way be?

An attempt at an answer can be given in brief review of the thesis of materialism as formulated in recent philosophy. This is the thesis that mental processes—sensations, emotions, and mental attitudes such as beliefs and wants—are in some sense identical with physical processes and events in the brain and with brain states. The thesis has been formulated in a variety of ways that elaborate on the early versions of the so-called "identity theory" of U. T. Place and J. J. C. Smart.[19] Both Place and Smart appeal to analogies between theoretical identities in the physical sciences and the mental-physical identity they advocate. We accept as true on empirical grounds such identities as 'Lightning is an electric discharge of type X', where 'X' is a description of a specific type of discharge, and 'Water is H_2O'. In them a term of ordinary language such as 'lightning' is combined with an abstract scientific term such as 'electric discharge'. The terms are taken from different language frameworks; they have different meanings; and the procedures by which we identify instances of them are very different. Yet we can combine them to form a meaningful identity which we accept as true. In the same way, it is argued, terms such as 'pain' and 'electro-chemical brain process of type X' can be combined to form the identity 'A pain is an electro-chemical brain process of type X'. 'Pain' as a term from ordinary language and the scientific term 'electro-chemical brain process' are from different language frameworks, as are also the rules governing their use. Certainly they differ in meaning, and have different criteria for their application. But it is argued this does not prevent us from asserting that they have the same referents any more than it does for theoretical identities.

Other formulations of the materialist thesis have not significantly altered the essentials of this argument. What is called "functionalism" disputes the claim that general "type-type" identities between the mental and physical can be stated. On the basis of their behavior we believe that lower animals and primitive creatures such as mollusks experience pain, yet their brain processes are very different from ours. We can also conceive of aliens from distant planets whose brain structures and composition are radically different from ours exhibiting pain behavior, grimacing when burnt by a fire or cut by a knife. Since no description of electro-chemical processes correlated to human pain would apply to the processes undergone by either the subhumans or aliens, we cannot assert an identity sentence relating such a physical description with the term 'pain'. Instead, the functionalists contend, mental events and states must be given abstract functional descriptions in terms of their causal relations to environmental stimuli, other mental events and states, and to behavior. A pain is the effect of a stimulus such as an intense irradiation, and the cause of future aversion to such stimuli and withdrawal behavior. Any process performing this same causal role can be identified with the pain, whatever specific description we give of this process.[20]

Functionalists claim to have replaced the type-type identities of earlier formulations with token-token identities. It is not pain as a type of mental event that is identified with a type of physical process, for it is this type that is given an abstract characterization in terms of functional relationships. We can only identify particular mental events and processes—the pain I now feel, the thought I am now having—with particular brain events and processes by using sentences stating token-token identities. But even this extent of revision is unnecessary. No arguments have been produced showing that species-specific mental processes cannot be identified with types of brain processes. It still remains plausible to maintain that human pain, if not pain in general, is identified with a specific process X to be discovered by future neurophysiology. The thesis of the identity between mental and physical thus remains, despite attempts at revision, the central thesis of contemporary materialism.

Its advocates have stressed that the thesis is not empirical. All that we can empirically establish is that there are correlations between mental and physical occurrences, e.g. that when a pain occurs, so does a characteristic brain process. But to speak of a correlation here presupposes two distinct entities, and this is what is advocated by dualist theories such as interactionism and parallelism. What then is the basis for the materialist thesis? Simplicity is often cited as an answer, the reasoning being that it would be simpler if there were one type of stuff, matter, instead of there being both mind and matter. But simplicity in itself is not a very strong reason. It would be simpler if there were one kind of elementary particle. But there are in fact a great variety of them. It would be simpler if there were a single virus that causes cancer, but in fact there are many. Often in the history of physics the simpler of competing theories has proven to be the one eventually accepted as true. But more often we find that nature exhibits great complexity and variety, and that simpler descriptions only distort. So it could also be with mental phenomena.

Another reason that can be given for materialism is the plausibility of the analogy between mental-physical identities and the theoretical identities of science. But there are important differences between the two. We have noted that theoretical identities such as 'Water is H_2O' and 'Lightning is an electric discharge' are based on the success of physical theories that are empirically testable, while mental-physical identities are nonempirical. Further, both pairs of terms 'water'-'H_2O' and 'lightning'-'electric discharge' are from the different language frameworks of ordinary and scientific discourse, but at least share the common function of having a standard descriptive use. In contrast, mental terms such as 'pain', 'belief', and 'want' have both first person and third person uses. I say both 'I have a pain' and 'He has a pain', 'I believe that p' and 'He believes that p', and 'I want E' and 'He wants E'. In all three cases the first person use is very different from that in the third person, having expressive and performative features that the third person use lacks. Given this contrast and the fact that it cannot be found for terms such as 'water' and 'H_2O', the analogy to the theoretical identities seems to be a weak one, certainly not sufficient upon which to base the case for materialism.

The best way to assess the identity thesis, however, is to determine what would follow it it were true. One possible consequence of terms such as 'human pain' and 'electro-chemical brain process of type X' having the same referents is that the former could be eliminated altogether from our vocabulary and replaced by the latter. The version of materialism known as "eliminative materialism" proposes just such an elimination and replacement. Just as the terms 'witch' and the 'phlogiston' of medieval science are now regarded as standing for fictions and, as the results of superstition and scientific ignorance, should hence be discarded from our working vocabulary, so terms such as 'pain' and 'belief' should eventually be eliminated, according to this version of materialism. In their place should be substituted the terms of neurophysiology that succeed in describing what does truly exist.

Could such an elimination and substitution possibly take place? There are strong reasons for thinking that they could not. When we use mental language both to report and express our own sensations and attitudes and to describe those of others we regard ourselves and our audience as part of a community engaged in mutual assistance and criticism. Those in our audience typically respond to our reports and expressions as we would ourselves. Thus, if I were to say to someone 'I am in pain', then normally that person would feel under some obligation to come to my assistance.

For me to describe another by saying 'He is in pain' is to regard that person as one who warrants my sympathy and assistance. To express a want by saying 'I want to leave now' may elicit from an audience preparations for my leaving, while for me to say of another 'He wants to leave' calls for a similar response from me and others. To express a belief by 'I believe it will rain' or describe one by 'He believes it will rain' is often to express or describe what is open to criticism or calls for justification. Should I or the other person hold that belief? For what reasons do we hold it? Such questions and subsequent inquiries are parts of the responses that the expressions and reports are liable to elicit. Even when we ascribe to lower animals sensations, wants, and expectations, we seem to regard them as also part of a shared community so far as they then become the objects of our sympathy and assistance.

Such attitudes and actions are, of course, lacking when we describe the events, processes, and states of affairs of our environment using our normal descriptive vocabulary. The descriptive statements 'I am 6 feet tall' or 'He weighs 150 pounds' imply no responses of sympathy, criticism, and assistance beyond simply a recognition that our audience and ourselves are part of a common speech community. They are the type of statements we would make in describing the height of a tree or the weight of a stone. Similar considerations apply to scientific descriptions of myself or others such as 'I am undergoing brain process X' or 'He is in brain state Y'. These are the type of statements that theoretical science could make about any process or state of affairs in nature, and imply none of the attitudes that are appropriate when first-person and third-person reports of sensations and psychological attitudes are used.

Given this fundamental difference between the uses of mental terms and the corresponding physical terms it seems entirely implausible that the latter could ever replace the former. Important social functions of the mental terms could not possibly be fulfilled by descriptions of brain processes or states. Eliminative materialism must therefore be rejected.

Many contemporary materialists may accept this conclusion, conceding that mental language will always have a role to perform. Nevertheless, they will claim that this role is inessential to the descriptive functions of our mental language, and it is these that are performed by physical descriptions. The claims of the identity theory and functionalism are directed only towards these descriptive functions, they will argue, as were the claims of the different varieties of dualism. We continue to use 'water' and 'lightning' as terms of our ordinary descriptive discourse which have sensible qualities among their criteria of application because for most purposes it is economical and convenient to do so. If the identity thesis were true, it would also be possible to justify the continued use of terms such as 'pain', 'believe', and 'want'. For "theoretical" purposes we could replace them by physical descriptions of brain processes and states, but such descriptions might be complex and their application understood only by those with special training in neurophysiology. For "practical" purposes of economy and ease of social communication it is convenient to retain the mental terms, realizing that they could be replaced for the "strict" scientific purposes of describing the physical world and that they lack referents distinct from those of the replacing physical descriptions.

We encountered the theoretical-practical distinction in Section 2.2 where we discussed the skeptics' attempt to deny "theoretical" certainty. Though its origin and motivation is different now, the use of the distinction is just as pernicious. As used by the materialist it implies that there is some external standard in terms of which we can judge the language framework of theoretical science superior for descriptive purposes to that of our framework of mental terms. It also implies that we can sharply demarcate the descriptive functions of language from the purposes to which they are put. Both implications are false. In Section 4.4 we saw how the purpose to which a given description is to be put determines the precision of the description and hence its information content. We judge the truth of a description relative to a given level of precision. A description of a brain process can be more precise than a first person report or third person description in which a mental term occurs. But there is no standard in terms of which we can evaluate the brain process description as true in a "strict" sense as compared to the mental description as merely an expedient approximation. All descriptions necessarily involve an essential element of expediency. Nor can these purposes be separated from the descriptive functions being performed. We use terms such as 'pain', 'believe', and 'want', as we have seen, within a context of mutual aid, sympathy, and criticism. They establish a communal bond between the speaker, his or her audience, and the person to whom they are ascribed. To use them descriptively is at the same time to perform these social functions. A brain process description, in contrast, would be used in the context of theoretical science as an institutionalized social specialization. The aims of this specialization are not in themselves those of aid, sympathy, and criticism, and hence its framework of discourse can dispense with the mental terminology of ordinary language. But there are no grounds for claiming that this framework has the priority claimed for it by the materialist thesis. On the contrary, the ends promoted by the mental language we use in our everyday lives seem to be even more fundamental than those served by theoretical science, since their satisfaction makes possible the cooperation essential for social specialization and science itself.

Notice how different this argument against materialism is from James's version of consequentialist pragmatism. If James were to reject materialism, he would have to base this rejection on the disadvantageous consequences that would follow from acting on the basis of it. This would be to regard the materialist thesis as a standard descriptive proposition to which the Consequentialist Condition applies. In contrast, materialism has been construed here as a thesis about language frameworks, either as a thesis proposing the replacement of our mental terminology with that of neurophysiology, as for eliminative materialism, or as a thesis permitting its retention but relegating its use to a secondary role justified by considerations of economy and ease of communication. If our argument against materialism is correct, neither the replacement nor the relegation can be justified. Replacement is impossible, since there are essential social functions that can be performed only by mental language. Relegation to a secondary role cannot be justified, since the mutual aid and criticism enabled by our mental language is essential for the development of science.

I hope these brief remarks are at least sufficient to indicate that, although pragmatic considerations are relevant to the evaluation of metaphysical propositions, they are relevant in a way very different from that for the empirical propositions we have been considering throughout the remainder of this work. Empirical propositions are formulated within a special type of discourse to which procedural rules of inquiry are relevant. Metaphysical propositions, in contrast, make claims about the scope and status of forms of discourse, claims very different from those of standard descriptive sentences. From this difference follows the unique relation that holds between them purposes.

Notes

Chapter 1 *Introduction*

1. The contrast between this language mediated interpretation and a "pure" kind is made in my *Principles of Semiotic* (London: Routledge & Kegan Paul, 1987), chap. 3. Accounts given in the semiotic tradition of natural signs fail to acknowledge this contrast.

2. See C. Hartshorne and P. Weiss, eds., *The Collected Papers of Charles Sanders Peirce*, 6 vols. (Cambridge: Harvard University Press, 1934–36), 2.330. A subject term, says Peirce, "denotes by prescribing what you are to do in order to gain a perceptual acquaintance with the object of the word."

3. David Hume, *A Treatise on Human Nature*, Bk. I, Pt. III, chap. XVI.

4. W. V. O. Quine and J. S. Ullian, *The Web of Belief* (New York: Random House, 1970), pp. 57, 58.

5. The form of practical inferences has been the subject of much controversy. For a review of alternative views see my *Practical Inferences* (London: Routledge & Kegan Paul, 1985), chaps. II and III. In this work I outline a variety of inferential forms, only one of which is presented in this summary account.

6. We are, of course, ignoring moral considerations in this discussion. The practical inferences being considered are exclusively prudential, those for which the wants and aversions of others can be considered as irrelevant. We also assume the agent has both the ability and opportunity to do *M*.

7. See my "On Distinguishing the 'Ought' from the 'Rational,' " *Philosophia* 15 (1985):251–70 for a more complete discussion of the differences between inferences to 'rational' and 'ought' conclusions. Here it is pointed out how liability to future correction serves to distinguish the latter. In making this distinction we must assume that 'ought' is not being used in what R. M. Hare has called its "inverted commas" sense.

8. Edna Ullman-Margalit, "On Presumption," *Journal of Philosophy* 80 (1983):143–63. A presumption, Ullman-Margalit says, enables us "to facilitate and expedite action. . . . It instructs its subjects to hold a certain proposition as true so as to have a foothold (as it were) for action. ...the intuition is this: given *p*, make *q* [the presumption] a premise in the rest of the pertinent piece of your practical reasoning."

9. For a discussion of the concept of plausibility see Douglas Odegard, *Knowledge and Skepticism* (Totowa: Rowman & Littlefield, 1982), pp. 6–16. Odegard proposes a "minimal concept" of plausibility requiring that a plausible hypothesis be not impossible or have some evidence in favor of it. This technical sense is contrasted with our ordinary, stronger sense in which the plausible is the reasonable, that which is favored by the available evidence.

10. These two types of acceptance correspond to the "acceptance₁" and "acceptance₂" outlined in Imre Lakatos, "Changes in the Problem of Inductive Logic" in *Philosophical Papers*, Vol. I, J. Worrall and G. Currie, eds. (Cambridge: Cambridge University Press, 1978). To accept₁ a hypothesis is for Lakatos to consider it as a candidate for acceptance₂ as something to the "worked on." For this same distinction between "tentative" and "full" acceptance of a proposition *P* see also Gilbert Harman, *Change in View* (Cambridge: MIT Press, 1986), pp. 46–50. Full acceptance, Harman says, ends further inquiry, and "one is *justified* in fully accepting only if one is justified in ending one's investigations whether *P* is true. This means one has to be justified in implicitly supposing that further investigation would not be sufficiently worthwhile."

11. *On Certainty*, translated by D. Paul and G. E. M. Anscombe (New York: Harper, 1969). The first passage is from Sec. 87, p. 13e, the second from Sec. 105, p. 16e.

12. The background knowledge of a person is also referred to by some writers as his "rational corpus" or "urcorpus." See Isaac Levi, *The Enterprise of Knowledge* (Cambridge: MIT Press, 1980), p. 13.

13. This is the central claim made in Saul Kripke's theory of proper names as "rigid designators" and his rejection of the description theories of Frege and Searle in *Naming and Necessity* (Cambridge: Harvard University Press, 1980), pp. 25–48. Kripke makes his claim in the context of determining the referent of a proper name. For this same theory of reference see Keith Donnellan, "Speaker Reference, Descriptions, and Anaphora" in P. French and H. Wettstein, eds., *Contemporary Perspectives in the Philosophy of Language* (Minneapolis: University of Minnesota Press, 1979).

14. For a discussion of the alcohol boiling point example see N. R. Hanson, *Patterns of Discovery* (Cambridge: Cambridge University Press, 1962), p. 97. Some modifications of this account must be made if the generalization is statistical. If we define an analytic sentence as one which is necessarily true, or true by definition, then 'All *S* is P_k is not analytic. For the argument that if *S* is a "law-cluster term," one which like 'alcohol' acquires meaning as the subject of accepted generalizations, it cannot be the subject of an analytic sentence see Hilary Putnam, "The Analytic and Synthetic" in H. Feigl and G. Maxwell, eds., *Minnesota Studies in the Philosophy of Science*, Vol. III (Minneapolis: University of Minnesota Press, 1962). Whether all the criteria expressed by a given subject *S* could be mistaken is a more difficult issue. Kripke and Putnam argue that the reference of *S* is that class of objects causally correlated with the term's original introduction, and that the only defining criteria for *S* are provided by the microphysical description of these objects. If successful, this argument would show that all later ascriptions could be false. See Kripke's *Naming and Necessity* and Putnam's "Is Semantics Possible?" in *Mind, Language and Reality* (Cambridge: Cambridge University Press, 1975).

15. The contrast drawn here is between what John Watkins calls a "naive" or "crude" fact and a "sophisticated" or "scientific" fact. See his *Science and Skepticism* (Princeton: Princeton University Press, 1984), pp. 262–72.

16. See Isaac Levi, "Truth, Fallibility and the Growth of Knowledge" in *Decisions and Revisions* (Cambridge: Cambridge University Press, 1984). "Our beliefs guide our conduct," Levi says, "by furnishing a criterion for distinguishing between logical possibilities which are serious and logical possibilities which are for all practical and theoretical purposes may be utterly ignored."

17. The term is introduced by Levi to stand for the view that conclusions accepted in science are to be justified by "scientific standards" and "judged in

terms of the institutional objectives of scientific inquiry." This view is contrasted with "behavioralism," the view that "the scientific propriety of a man's beliefs is dependent, at least in part, on the moral, political, economic, etc. consequences of having these beliefs." See *Gambling with Truth* (New York: Knopf, 1967), pp. 16, 17. The term 'cognitivism' is also applied to theories of practical deliberation that attempt to replace the expressions of wants as the first premises of practical inferences with evaluations of the desirability of what is wanted. For a discussion of these theories of what can be called *practical cognitivism* (as contrasted with the *epistemic cognitivism* considered here) see my *Practical Inferences,* chap. IV.

18. *Collected Papers,* 5.589.

19. *Knowledge and Human Interests* (1968), translated by J. J. Shapiro (Boston: Beacon Press, 1971), p. 195. The date in parentheses is that of the original German edition.

20. In his defense of pragmatism Richard Rudner clearly distinguishes both issues from that with which he is dealing. See his "The Scientist Qua Scientist Makes Value Judgments," *Philosophy of Science* 20 (1953):1–6.

CHAPTER 2   *Knowledge and Rational Belief*

1. *Theaetetus,* 201.

2. Keith Lehrer, "The Doxastic System and Complete Justification" in *Knowledge* (London: Oxford University Press, 1974).

3. The formulation of the example that follows is from Lehrer's "Knowledge, Truth, and Evidence" in *Knowing: Essays in the Analysis of Knowledge,* M. D. Roth and L. Gallis, eds. (New York: Random House, 1970). Gettier's original example is in "Is Justified True Belief Knowledge?," *Analysis* 23 (1963):121–23.

4. For a survey of these attempts see Robert K. Shope, *The Analysis of Knowing* (Princeton: Princeton University Press, 1983).

5. See especially Alvin I. Goldman, "A Causal Theory of Knowledge" in *Essays on Knowledge and Justification,* G. Pappas and M. Swain, eds. (Ithaca: Cornell University Press, 1978). For Goldman, X's justified belief in someone owning a Ford in the example of the preceding paragraph does not constitute knowledge because the belief is not caused by Havit's owning a Ford.

6. See D. S. Mannison, " 'Inexplicable Knowledge' Does Not Require Belief," *Philosophical Quarterly* 26 (1976):139–48 and Merrill Ring, "Knowledge: The Cessation of Belief," *American Philosophical Quarterly* 14 (1977):51–9. For the argument that the stronger certainty condition is not essential see Colin Radford, "Knowledge - By Examples," Analysis 27 (1966):1–11.

7. See J. L. Austin, "Other Minds" in *Philosophical Papers,* J. O. Urmson and G. J. Warnock, eds. (Oxford: Clarendon Press, 1961).

8. For a discussion of this sense see Paul Ziff's *Epistemic Analysis* (Dordrecht, D. Reidel, 1984), pp. 57–60.

9. Keith Lehrer and Thomas D. Paxson, Jr., "Knowledge: Undefeated Justified True Belief" in *Essays on Knowledge and Justification,* Pappas and Swain, eds. The same criticism levelled here against Lehrer and Paxson seems applicable also to Goldman's "Discrimination and Perceptual Knowledge" in the same volume. For perceptual knowledge that p Goldman requires that there be no "perceptual equivalents" that would produce the belief that p. A "perceptual equivalent" for a person is defined as some relevant state of affairs that that person could not discriminate from the actual perceived state of affairs producing the belief. As for Lehrer and Paxson's defeators, it would seem impossible for us

to ever determine whether or not there are such perceptual equivalents in a given situation and on this basis determine knowledge.

10. A. J. Ayer, *The Problem of Knowledge* (Baltimore: Penguin Books, 1956), p. 35.

11. Peter Unger, *Ignorance* (Oxford: Clarendon Press, 1975), p. 39.

12. The practical-absolute distinction outlined here has been made by many writers. For discussions of it relative to perceptual propositions see Norman Malcom, "The Verification Argument" in his Knowledge and Certainty (Englewood Cliffs: Prentice-Hall, 1962) and Harry Frankfurt, "Philosophical Certainty," *Philosophical Review* 71 (1962):303–32. For discussions of the distinction relative to the certainty of empirical generalizations see Henry E. Kyburg, Jr., *Probability and Inductive Logic* (London: Macmillan, 1970), pp. 110, 111 and Karl Popper, *Objective Knowledge* (Oxford: Clarendon Press, 1972), p. 79. Both Kyburg and Popper endorse the skeptical conclusion that we can have practical certainty, but absolute certainty is unattainable.

13. The contrast between "invariant" and "contextual" interpretations of terms such as 'flat' and 'certain' can be found in Unger's *Philosophical Relativity* (Minneapolis: University of Minnesota Press, 1983), pp. 6–11. It is the invariant interpretation of 'certain' as standing for an absolute limit, Unger argues here, that leads directly to skepticism.

14. Still the best summary of this Wittgensteinian criticism of skepticism is to be found in Malcom's "Moore and Ordinary Language" in P. Schilpp, ed., *The Philosophy of G. E. Moore* in *The Library of Living Philosophers*, Vol. IV (La Salle: Open Court, 1942).

15. To deny this view of the first person use of 'certain', Ayer claims that to be convinced or certain of a proposition "does not seem to consist in any special mental occurrence. It is rather a matter of accepting the fact in question and of not being at all disposed to doubt it than of contemplating it with a conscious feeling of conviction." See *The Problem of Knowledge,* p. 12. Ayer's view can be contrasted to that expressed by Russell when he claims that a belief is "constituted by a certain feeling or complex of sensations, attached to the content believed." See Bertrand Russell, *The Analysis of Mind* (London: Allen and Unwin, 1921), p. 250.

16. Philosophers do speak of an "occurrent" beliefs, but what they seem to be invariably referring to are dateable acts of acceptance.

17. Gilbert Ryle, *The Concept of Mind* (New York: Barnes and Noble, 1949), chaps. II and V.

18. Saul Kripke, "A Puzzle About Belief" in *Meaning and Use,* A. Margalit, ed. (Dordrecht: D. Reidel, 1976). Kripke adds the condition that X be a "normal" speaker of English and that he sincerely assent to '*p*' "on reflection."

19. Robert Stalnaker, *Inquiry* (Cambridge: MIT Press, 1984), p. 93. A different reason for rejecting the principle has also been given by defenders of instrumentalist theories of science. Arthur Fine notes for van Fraasen's version of instrumentalism that a theory is accepted as true if it is empirically adequate relative to observed data, but this does not require belief in the existence of the entities postulated by the theory. See his "Unnatural Attitudes: Realist and Instrumentalist Attachments to Science," *Mind* 95 (1986):49–79. This objection seems to confuse, however, belief in the truth of a theory with belief that its referential presuppositions are satisfed. There seems to be no inconsistency between believing electromagnetic theory to be true and believing that a theoretical term such as 'magnetic field' occurring in the formulation of the theory lacks a referent.

20. For the view that evaluation is inapplicable to beliefs see William Alston, "Concepts of Epistemic Justification," *Monist* 68 (1985):57–83. Obligations do not directly apply to beliefs, Alston argues, but we can apply them indirectly "on the model of the way in which obligations bear on various other conditions over which one lacks direct voluntary control but which one can influence by voluntary actions." That beliefs are held involuntarily is argued for by Bernard Williams in "Deciding to Believe" in *Problems of the Self* (Cambridge: Cambridge University Press, 1973).

21. This model was first proposed by David Armstrong in *Belief, Truth and Knowledge* (Cambridge: Cambridge University Press, 1979), pp. 166–171. The reliabilist theory of justification is advanced by Alvin Goldman in "Discrimination and Perceptual Knowledge," *Journal of Philosophy* 73 (1976):771–91 and "What is Justified Belief?" *in Justification and Knowledge*, G. S. Pappas, ed. (Dordrecht: D. Reidel, 1979). In this latter volume Michael Swain in "Justification and the Basis of Belief" endorses a version that he refers to as the "probability-reliability" model of epistemic justification.

22. How to specify the beliefs entering into such causal relations is one of the central problems of the discipline known as "cognitive science." For the so-called "sentential theory" to have a belief is to have a token of the sentence expressing the belief's content encoded in one's brain, and it is this brain state that functions as a term in causal relations. For a discussion of this theory see Steven Stich, *From Folk Psychology to Cognitive Science* (Cambridge, MIT Press, 1983).

23. This problem of relevant types is discussed in Richard Feldman, "Reliability and Justification," *Monist* 68 (1985):159–74 and Alvin Plantinga, "Epistemic Justification," *Nous* 20 (1986):3–18. Specification of types includes also specification of the state of the visual receptors of the subject, his state of fatigue, etc., factors that are ignored in the simple example that follows.

24. Goldman, "Discrimination and Perceptual Knowledge" in *Epistemology and Cognition* (Cambridge: Harvard University Press, 1983), chap. 3.

25. Swain proposes in "Justification and the Basis of Belief" that we require only that the belief have a probability of success in the same type of conditions higher than for any competing belief. In the case of 'This is red' the competing beliefs might be beliefs in 'This is yellow', 'This is orange', etc. But this would allow us to assess rationality for a belief in redness if it had a probability of .55 of success in contrast to a belief in orange with probability of .54, and this seems implausible.

26. Nils-Eric Sahlin in " 'How to be 100% Certain 99.5% of the Time'," *Journal of Philosophy* 83 (1986):91–111.

27. This sustaining requirement seems first stated by Armstrong in *Belief, Truth and Knowledge*, pp. 77ff as a condition for a person having "conclusive" reasons for a belief. Armstrong concedes that such a condition has no relevance as whether the person has "good" reasons for the belief.

28. See Robert Audi, "The Causal Structure of Indirect Justification," *Journal of Philosophy* 80 (1983):398–415. Audi is responding to Lehrer's example in *Knowledge*, pp. 124, 125 of a gypsy lawyer who believes in his client's innocence because of a reading of tarot cards, though he has independent evidence that provide logical grounds for the client's innocence. If the tarot cards' basis were removed, the lawyer would cease to believe in this innocence, despite the independent evidence. In Audi's view the lawyer has no personal justification for his belief, since it is not caused by the evidence that logically supports it.

CHAPTER 3   *Induction and Logical Probability*

1. In cases of causal overdetermination A will not be necessary for B and the logical formulation of the causal relation between A and B is more complex. For the analysis of a cause as an insufficient part of an unnecessary but sufficient condition, or what he terms an "inus condition," see John Mackie, *The Cement of the Universe* (Oxford: Clarendon Press, 1974), chap. 3. For a discussion and proposed amendment to Mackie's formulation of this inus condition see Theodore Denise, "On the Nature of INUS Conditionality," *Analysis* 44 (1984):49–52.

2. The term 'retroduction' was introduced by Peirce. See his *Collected Papers*, 2.706–08, 2.755. Peirce also uses 'abduction' for this mode of inference. For a more recent account of this mode of inference see Hanson's *Patterns of Scientific Discovery*, pp. 85–92.

3. At the theoretical level, conclusive falsification is difficult because of the possibility of introducing auxiliary hypotheses and reinterpreting experimental data in order to "save" a hypothesis. For an acknowledgement of this and the proposal that a falsification is decisive only when it is confirming instance of an alternative theory with increased explanatory power see Imre Lakatos, "Falsification and the Methodology of Scientific Research Programmes" in Criticism and the Growth of Knowledge, Lakatos and A. Musgrave, eds. (Cambridge: Cambridge University Press, 1970).

4. A similar criticism of Popper's view has been made by a number of writers. See, for example, Wesley Salmon, *The Foundations of Scientific Inference* (Pittsburgh: Pittsburgh University Press, 1966), pp. 26–28.

5. For the wider sense of 'evidence' including all background knowledge see Kyburg, *Probability and the Logic of Rational Belief,* pp. 81–85. It is, of course, impossible to distinguish background knowledge used in interpreting observations from the more restricted sense of 'evidence' adopted here, for how we describe what we observe is a function of this background. Evidence as a term of a logical relation consists of these descriptions. It is the difficulty of distinguishing evidence from background knowledge, especially at the theoretical level, which has lead to the popularity of coherence theories of knowledge.

6. It is this type of justification that F. L. Will seems to be contrasting to the absence of a justification for induction in general in "Generalization and Evidence" in *Philosophical Analysis,* M. Black, ed. (Englewood Cliffs: Prentice Hall, 1963).

7. J. M. Keynes states this as the principle "that the amount of variety in the universe is limited in such a way that there is no one object so complex that its qualities fall into an infinite number of independent groups." See *A Treatise on Probability* (London, Macmillan, 1921), p. 258. G. H. von Wright in *The Logical Problem of Induction*, 2nd ed. (Oxford: Blackwell, 1957). Pp. 76–84 also employ this principle.

8. Cf. Carnap in *Logical Foundations of Probability* (Chicago, University of Chicago Press, 1950), p. 493: "A sample is called a random sample if it has been selected from the population by a procedure of such a kind that...in the prolonged application of the procedure all individuals will be selected with equal frequencies."

9. This interpretation of Mill's method of agreement as the elimination of hypotheses stating that given factors are necessary conditions and the method of agreement as the elimination of potential sufficient conditions is due to von Wright. See his *The Logical Problem of Induction,* pp. 73–75.

10. For a discussion of Popper's concept of stringency relative to historical examples see Watkins, *Science and Skepticism,* pp. 292–303.

11. Here we are regarding the inference as non-deductive. Qualifications must be introduced if it is claimed to be deductive. As formulated within the frequency theory the rule allows us to infer to the qualified conclusion that an *A* will be *B* with probability $m/n \pm \delta$, where δ is a rational number that is an interval of possible error. The theory stipulates that δ will approach zero as the number *n* in the sample is indefinitely increased. This follows from the definition of probability in the frequency theory as the limit of relative frequency for an infinitely large sample or infinitely long sequence of trials. For the formulation of this rule see Hans Reichenbach, *The Theory of Probability*, translated by E. Hutton and M. Reichenbach (Berkeley, University of California Press, 1949), p. 446. In the classical theory an even more qualified conclusion is stated. The probability $p(B/A) = r \pm \delta$ is regarded as itself having a probability *P* of stating the proportion of *A*s which are in fact *B* which is equal to $1-\epsilon$, where ϵ is the interval of possible error. As the number of individuals in the sample approaches infinity, *P* approaches to 1 (or ϵ approaches 0).

12. The actual calculation of posterior probabilities by Bayes' Theorem is carried out by comparing two or more hypotheses relative to evidence. Let H_U be the hypothesis that the coin is unbiased, i.e. that $p(B/A) = .5$, to which we continue to assign a prior probability of .9, i.e. $p(H_U) = .9$. Let H_B be the hypothesis that the coin is biased to the extent that it will turn up heads on 4 out of 5 trials, i.e. that $p(B/A) = .8$, and let us assign to this the prior probability of .1, or $p(H_B) = .1$. Suppose we have a sequence of 3 tosses, all of which turn up heads. The probability of this event *E* relative to H_u is $.5 \times .5 \times .5 = .125$, or $p(E/H_u) = .125$. Relative to H_B the probability of *E* is $.8 \times .8 \times .8 = .512$, or $p(E/H_B) = .512$. Then the posterior probability of H_u, or $p(H_u/E)$, is given by Bayes' Theorem as equal to

$$\frac{p(H_u) \times p(E/H_u)}{p(H_u) \times p(E/H_u) + p(H_B) \times p(E/H_B)}$$

$$= \frac{.9 \times .125}{(.9 \times .125) + (.1 \times .512)} = \frac{.113}{.163} = .69$$

Similarly, $p(H_B/E) = \dfrac{.1 \times .512}{(.9 \times .125) + (.1 \times .512)} = \dfrac{.05}{.163} = .31$

The effect of the sequence of three heads is thus to somewhat lower the probability of the unbiased hypothesis H_u from .9 to .69, while raising the probability of H_B from .1 to .31. A longer sequence in which heads predominate will have the effect of further lowering the probability of H_u. In general, for *k* number of alternative hypotheses $H_1, H_2, \ldots, H_k$ Bayes' Theorem states that for any *i*th hypothesis H_i

$$p(H_i/E) = \frac{p(H_i) \times p(E/H_i)}{\sum_{j=1}^{k} p(H_j) \times p(E/H_j)}$$

13. For an outline of this theory and some criticisms of its assumptions see Henry Kyburg, Jr., *Probability and the Logic of Belief* (Middlebury: Wesleyan University Press, 1961), pp. 34–38 and "Subjective Probability" in *Epistemology and Inference* (Minneapolis: University of Minnesota Press, 1983), pp. 79–98. The classical source for the theory is Leonard Savage, *The Foundations of Statistics*, 2nd ed. (New York: Dover, 1972).

14. For some of these criticisms see Roy Weatherford, *Philosophical Foundations of Probability Theory* (London, Routledge & Kegan Paul), 1982, p. 119.

15. Kyburg, *Probability and the Logic of Belief*, p. 102.

16. Reichenbach, *The Theory of Probability*, p. 441. Deciding on the extent to which attributes are to be varied is similar to deciding what Reichenbach calls the "weight of an evidence," which "is to be interpreted as the result of previous inductions, all of which are ultimately reducible to induction by enumeration."

17. Kyburg, *The Probability and the Logic of Rational Belief*, p. 5. This logical interpretation of probability is due to Keynes. See *A Treatise on Probability*, pp. 3ff.

18. For the detailed development of these methods see Carnap's *Logical Foundations of Probability and The Continuum of Inductive Methods* (Chicago: University of Chicago Press, 1952).

19. In general, for every sentence with n propositional constituents there will be 2^n possible interpretations. The prior logical probability r' will be equal to $w/2^n$, where w is what Carnap terms ϕ's *width*, the number of possible interpretations in which it is true. Carnap formulates this equation in terms of atomic propositions distinguished into names $a_1, a_2, ..., a_n$ of objects and predicates $P_1, P_2, ..., P_m$. For m predicates and n named objects the number of constituents of a given ϕ will be $m \times n$. Hence, $r' = w/2^{mxn}$. See *The Continuum of Inductive Methods*, pp. 42–44.

20. See Jaako Hintikka, "On a Combined System of Inductive Logic," *Acta Philosophica Fennica* 18 (1965):21–30 and "Towards a Theory of Inductive Generalizations" in *Logic, Methodology and Philosophy of Science*, Y. Bar-Hillel, ed. (Amsterdam: N. Holland, 1965). Hintikka criticizes Carnap's method for determining degrees of confirmation for uniform generalizations because it leads to the implausible result that all have the value zero where the population is infinitely large. This feature is also criticized by Ernest Nagel in "Carnap's Theory of Induction" in *The Philosophy of Rudolph Carnap*, Vol. XI of *The Library of Living Philosophers*, P. Schilpp, ed. (LaSalle: Open Court, 1963). The summary I give greatly simplifies Hintikka's exposition of his method of assigning probabilities.

21. For an exposition of this technique of analyzing into existence-constituents (originally due to Herbrand and developed by von Wright) see my *Deductive Logic*, Carbondale, Southern Illinois University Press, 1974. In general, for m predicates there will be 2^m existence-constituents for which there will be 2^{2^m} possible interpretations. If we exclude the empty domain (a complication that I ignore above) this number is reduced by one.

22. See Kyburg, *Probability and the Logic of Rational Belief*, pp. 22, 23 and *Probability and Inductive Logic* (London: Macmillan, 1970), pp. 48–50. The same criticism is made by A. J. Ayer in *Probability and Evidence* (New York: Columbia University Press, 1950), p. 62. The fact that for the frequency theory probabilities are limits of relative frequencies in infinite sequences leads R. von Mises, the original formulator of the theory, to claim that probabilities of single events are "without the sort of meaning appropriate to the probability calculus." "The phrase 'probability of death', when it refers to a single person," von Mises claims, "has no meaning at all for us." See his *Probability, Statistics, and Truth* (New York: Macmillan, 1957), p. 11, the English translation of *Wahrescheinlichkeit, Statistik, und Wahrkeit* (Berlin: J. Springer, 1928). The same view is advanced by Reichenbach, for whom individual probabilities have a "fictitious meaning" and are stated in an "elliptical mode of speech" by transferring meaning from the general to the individual case. This transfer is justifiable, not for cognitive reasons, he says, but "because it serves the practice of action to deal with such statements as meaningful." See *The Theory of Probability*, p. 377.

This contrast between "cognitive reasons" and the "practice of action" is typical of cognitivist theories.

23. Reichenbach, *The Theory of Probability*, pp. 374–79. See also Ayer, "Two Notes on Probability" in *The Concept of a Person* (New York: St. Martin's, 1963).

24. Indeed, in Levi's formulation of a direct inference the assignment of a degree of confirmation is made the conclusion of the inference. See his "Direct Inference" in *Decisions and Revisions* (Cambridge: Cambridge University Press, 1984). Levi's "solution" to the problem of the reference class is to require that the individual a_i be selected on the same basis as those in the sample.

25. "The Aim of Inductive Logic" in *Logic, Methodology and Philosophy of Science*, E. Nagel, P. Suppes, and A. Tarski, eds. (Stanford: Stanford University Press, 1962). This view has also been defended by Richard Jeffrey. The scientist, says Jeffrey, "should refrain from accepting or rejecting hypotheses," leaving this for policy makers faced with specific decisions. The scientist's proper role is only "to provide the rational agents in the society which he represents with probabilities for...hypotheses." See his "Valuation and Acceptance of Scientific Hypotheses," *Philosophy of Science* 23 (1956):237–46.

26. *Logical Foundations of Probability*, pp. 251, 252. Similar reasoning is used by Reichenbach when he refers to individual probabilities as "posits," with the "weight" of the posit derived from a statistical generalization by way of a direct inference. See *The Theory of Probability*, pp. 377ff.

27. Among advocates of these versions should be listed Kyburg and Levi. Kyburg adopts the skeptical strategy of distinguishing between "practical" and "absolute" certainty, and argues that it is only in the former sense that we can set a level of confirmation for acceptance. See *Probability and Inductive Logic*, pp. 110, 111. For Levi's version see *Gambling with Truth*, pp. 76ff. Ayer also claims in *Probability and Evidence*, p. 87 that "it is rational to accept a generalization when it has acquired a high degree of instance confirmation, without meeting any counter-instance." Carnap formulates a number of alternative rules of acceptance in *Logical Foundations of Probability*, pp. 255–269, though the decision to accept is for him made only by the decision-maker relative to an action whose consequences can be assigned specific utilities.

28. Roderick Chisholm, *Perceiving* (Ithaca: Cornell University Press, 1957), pp. 10, 11.

29. Ibid., p. 9.

30. A similar standard is set by Carl Hempel, though he requires $c(h/e)$ to be greater than $\frac{1}{2}$ for rational acceptance. If $c(h/e) = \frac{1}{2}$, Hempel says, h may be accepted, rejected, or left in suspense. See "Deductive Nomological vs. Statistical Explanation" in *Minnesota Studies in the Philosophy of Science*, Vol. III, H. Feigl and G. Maxwell, eds. Hempel also requires consideration of "epistemic utility" in common with advocates of an acceptance rule to be presently considered.

31. This formulation of the paradox is due to Kyburg in "Conjunctivitis" in *Induction, Acceptance and Rational Belief*, M. Swain, ed. (Dordrecht: D. Reidel, 1969). To resolve the paradox and still retain probabilities as acceptance thresholds Kyburg makes the implausible proposal that we abandon the requirement to accept a conjunction if the conjuncts are accepted. See also Carnap, *Logical Foundations of Probability*, p. 256.

32. Lehrer states a criterion for "completely justified" belief, one part of which incorporates this rule, another part Chisholm's weak acceptance rule. In order to be completely justified in believing a proposition p, he maintains, p must

be "believed to have a better chance of being true than the denial of *p* or any other statement that competes with *p*." See *Knowledge*, p. 198.

33. The "epistemic utility" of a hypothesis is defined as a function of its degree of confirmation and level of information content, and rules are formulated for selecting hypotheses on the basis of both standards. For such an attempt see Levi, *Gambling with Truth*, pp. 76, 77, where a high information content or "degree of relief from agnosticism" in addition to confirmation by evidence is said to be a criterion for hypothesis selection. For Levi acceptance is also a function of the "degree of caution" exercised by an investigator as his aversion to error. But as Levi admits, this is a psychological, subjective factor, and seems irrelevant to the normative question whether a given hypothesis *ought* to be accepted. Lehrer also claims that the "reasonableness of accepting a proposition is a function of our interest in [information] content and our interest in avoiding error. The two objectives must be balanced against the other." See his "The Gettier Problem and the Analysis of Knowledge."

CHAPTER 4 *The Pragmatist Alternative*

1. "On the Applications of Inductive Logic," *Philosophy and Phenomenological Research* 8 (1947):133–47. The same principle is advanced by Russell when he states that the premisses for inductive inferences should embrace "all the relevant evidence." See *Human Knowledge* (New York: Simon and Schuster, 1948), p. 498.

2. *Probability and Inductive Logic*, p. 169. The question "when to stop gathering evidence is a pragmatic one," Kyburg adds, which is irrelevant for assigning probabilities and acceptance.

3. *Perceiving*, p. 27.

4. For this criticism of Carnap's principle see Ayer, "Two Notes on Probability" in *The Concept of a Person* (New York: St. Martin's, 1963).

5. Cf. C. I. Lewis in *The Ground and Nature of the Right* (New York: Columbia University Press, 1955), p. 322: "No inductive conclusion is well taken and justly credible unless the obligation to muster the given and available evidence has been met." Ayer in "Two Notes on Probability" also suggests that the Principle of Total Evidence be "defined by reference not to the results of all the relevant observations that one happens to have made, but to those of all the relevant observations that one could make if one chose." But he notes that there is almost always an indefinite number of such relevant observations, and without a way of terminating the search for more evidence this interpretation of the principle is "of little practical use."

6. Cf. Lehrer, *Knowledge*, p. 105: "Perceptual beliefs are considered innocent until proven guilty when we care not the least whether the belief is innocent or guilty. Once we do care, though, then we start to ask serious questions."

7. M. C. Weinstein and H. V. Fineberg, *Clinical Decision Analysis* (Philadelphia: W. B. Saunders, 1980), p. 1. I am grateful to Eugenia Gatens-Robinson for bringing this example to my attention.

8. Gilbert Harman, "Reasoning and Evidence One Does not Possess" in *Midwest Studies in Philosophy*, Vol. V (Minneapolis: University of Minnesota Press, 1980). An earlier version of this same example can be found also in Harman's *Thought* (Princeton: Princeton University Press, 1973), pp. 120ff. In this latter work Harman poses the same problem of unpossessed evidence relative to Lehrer and Paxson's example of a subject seeing a man Tom Grabit stealing a

book from a library and apparently knowing that Tom Grabit is the thief, but being unaware of Mrs. Grabit's misleading testimony that Tom's identical twin was the thief. See also John Barker, "What You Don't Know Won't Hurt You?", *American Philosophical Quarterly* 13 (1976):303–08 for the view that the more readily available the evidence that remains unconsidered by the subject the less we are inclined to grant him knowledge. Such examples are summarized in Shope's *The Analysis of Knowing*, pp. 225ff.

9. Catherine Lowry points out in "Gettier's Notion of Justification," *Mind* 87 (1978):105–8 that the range of Gettier examples can be restricted severely if we require for justified belief that "no more can reasonably be expected of him with respect to finding out whether the proposition is true." In virtually all Gettier examples of the kind discussed above in Section 2.1 there is some potentially defeating evidence that is available to the subject and could be acquired if sufficient effort were made.

10. William Lycan, "Evidence One Does Not Possess," *Australasian Journal of Philosophy* 55 (1977):114–26. For a discussion of Harman's example and others related to it see also R. Foley and R. Fumerton, "Epistemic Indolence," *Mind* 91 (1982):38–56.

11. It is the consideration of such factors that leads David Annis to conclude that knowledge claims must be assessed "relative to some specific issue-context which determines the level of understanding and knowledge required." See "A Contextualist Theory of Epistemic Justification," *American Philosophical Quarterly* 15 (1978):213–19. See also Paul Ziff's *Epistemic Analysis*, p. 159: "If the gravity of a claim is minimal we are prepared to tolerate an increased risk [of error]: the requirements for knowing that *p* are, accordingly, relaxed."

12. For the argument to this conclusion see my *Practical Inferences*, chap. 4.

13. The standard method of assigning numerical measures of utilities in terms of preferences between certain outcomes and lotteries is due to von Neumann and Morgenstern. For an exposition of it, as well as a discussion of some of its difficulties, see R. D. Luce and H. Raiffa, *Games and Decisions* (New York: Wiley, 1967).

14. I am grateful to Richard Fumerton for these examples.

15. An early anticipation of this condition can be found in the writings of Bernard Bolzano. Bolzano defines the "danger" to which we are subject when not prepared for the truth of a proposition as the product of the damage we would suffer if it were true and the probability of this occurring. For a *p* to be "morally certain" seems to mean for him that we are justified in accepting *p*, and "whether or not a proposition is morally certain depends on the magnitude of damage that would result if its opposite came about and we were unprepared for it, and on other circumstances as well." In common with philosophers of the cognitivist tradition Bolzano distinguishes moral certainty from the "proper certainty" (what later is called "absolute" or "theoretical" certainty) required for science. See *Theory of Science* (1837), translated by R. George (Oxford: Blackwell, 1972), p. 362.

16. This objection is stated in Watkins, *Science and Skepticism*, p. 38.

17. For Abraham Wald decisions about how many observations should be made during the whole course of experimentation are decisions about the design of an experiment and are made prior to beginning the testing of a hypothesis h. By distinguishing these decisions from "terminal decisions" to accept or reject *h* he successfully avoids the objection just raised. But the effect of separating terminal decisions from design decisions is to mistakenly separate the former

from costs of acquiring evidence. See his *Statistical Decision Functions,* 2nd ed. (New York: Chelsea, 1971), p. 19.

18. See Isaac Levi, "On the Seriousness of Mistakes" and "Must the Scientist Make Value Judgments?", both in *Decisions and Revisions.* For the argument that hypotheses in science are accepted with an indefinite number of applications for which costs of a mistake cannot possibly be calculated see Jeffrey's "Valuation and Acceptance of Scientific Hypotheses."

19. *Collected Papers,* 5.602. Two paragraphs earlier (5.600) Peirce states a more qualified pragmatic condition for provisional acceptance, saying that postponement of the testing of a hypothesis may be brought about when the likelihood of it being false "is of an unmistakenly objective character, and is supported by good inductions." Here economy considerations are a "leading factor," but apparently for him not the only factor.

20. Lakatos, "Falsification and the Methodology of Scientific Research Programmes."

21. For an analysis of questions and their presuppositions see N. Belnap and T. Steele, *The Logic of Questions and Answers* (New Haven: Yale University Press, 1976).

22. Isaac Levi, "Information and Inference" in *Decisions and Revisions.*

23. A specific application of this feature of information is presented by explanations as answers to "why" questions. For the pragmatic theory of explanation developed by van Fraasen an explanation is always relevant to the interests of those posing such a question. For the contrast between this view and an "ontic" theory holding there is a single "ideally complete" explanation for a given phenomenon in terms of underlying causal mechanisms see van Fraasen's "Salmon on Explanation," *Journal of Philosophy* 82 (1985):639–51.

24. See *The Logic of Scientific Discovery,* Secs. 31, 35.

25. The importance of these investigations for epistemology was first noted by Alvin Goldman in "Epistemics: The Regulative Theory of Cognition," *Journal of Philosophy* 75 (1978):509–23.

26. The results of these studies are summarized in E. E. Smith and D. L. Medlin, *Categories and Concepts* (Cambridge: Harvard University Press, 1980). Categorization in them included both identifying particular objects as belonging to a given species or genus and categorizing a given species within a genus, e.g. categorizing a robin as a bird. Only the former is of interest to us here.

27. The schema becomes then what Smith and Medlin term a "template" as a "relational gestalt." See *Categories and Concepts,* pp. 130–40. They note that matching to an iconic schema can be employed as an identification procedure only for those terms applied to concrete objects. For a comparison of these iconic schemas to Kant's representations of the imagination see Mark Johnson, *The Body and the Mind* (Chicago: University of Chicago Press, 1987), chap. 6.

28. See R. Nisbett and L. Ross, *Human Inference* (Englewood Cliffs: Prentice Hall, 1980) for a review of these studies and a discussion of their implications and also A. Tversky and D. Kahneman's title lead essay in D. Kahneman, P. Slovic, A. Tversky, eds., *Judgment Under Uncertainty: Heuristics and Biases (Cambridge:* Cambridge University Press, 1982).

29. Harman, *Change in View,* p. 50: "If one had unlimited powers of record keeping and an unlimited ability to survey ever more complex structures of arguments, replies, rebuttals, and so on, it would be rational always to accept things only tentatively as working hypotheses, never ending inquiry." This would be true, however, only if this "unlimited ability" meant that a survey carried with it no costs, and this is never the case.

30. *Human Inference,* p. 3. This point is emphasized again on p. 255 where they note the cost of everyday intuitive strategies "is generally so low, relative to more formal strategies, that it seems distinctly possible that the long-range 'economics' of their habitual, preferential use is well in balance...of their disadvantageous consequences." See also Hilary Kornblith, "Justified Belief and Epistemically Responsible Action," *Philosophical Review* 92 (1983):33–48 for the view that departures from norms of "ideal reasoning" can nonetheless be justified as "epistemically responsible."

31. *Human Inference,* p. 189.

32. *Human Inference,* p. 191.

33. Feyerabend, *Against Method* (Highlands, Humanities, 1975), p. 28: "There is only *one* principle that can be defended under *all* circumstances and in *all* stages of human development. It is the principle: *anything goes.*"

CHAPTER 5 *Varieties of Pragmatism*

1. *Collected Papers,* 5.402.

2. Ibid., 5.403.

3. Ibid., 5.406. My interpretation of Peirce relies on that given by Karl-Otto Apel in *Charles S. Peirce,* translated by J. M. Kraus, (Amherst: University of Massachusetts Press, 1981), pp. 25ff.

4. *Collected Papers,* 5.407.

5. Cf. Ayer, *The Origins of Pragmatism* (San Fransisco: Freeman and Cooper, 1968), p. 16. Here he notes that for Peirce "the distinction between what is true and what we believe to be true is one to which we cannot ourselves give any practical bearing."

6. For the classic statement of this theory originally due to Frank Ramsay see P. F. Strawson's "Truth" in *Logico-Linguistic Papers* (London: Methuen, 1971).

7. This point is elaborated more fully in my *Principles of Semiotic,* Section 5.3. It is Strawson's inability to distinguish between the conventional and nonconventional that seems to be a central reason for Austin's rejection of the redundancy theory in "Truth" in his *Philosophical Papers* (Oxford: Clarendon Press, 1961).

8. John Dewey, *Logic, The Theory of Inquiry* (New York: Holt, 1938). With his characteristic carelessness Dewey seems to equate knowledge with truth, and then claims that knowledge is related to inquiry as its "warrantably assertible product" (p. 118). But he also notes that "in scientific inquiry, the criterion of what is taken to be settled, or to be knowledge, is being *so* settled that it is available as a resource in further inquiry; not being settled in such a way as not to be subject to revision in further inquiry" (pp. 8,9). Richard Rorty discusses Dewey's theory in his popularization of pragmatism in *Consequences of Pragmatism* (Minneapolis: University of Minnesota Press, 1982), pp. xxv-xxix.

9. See *Reason, Truth and History* (Cambridge: Cambridge University Press, 1981), p. 55.

10. This passage from *Pragmatism* (New York: Longmans and Green, 1907), p. 218 seems to indicate an application to all descriptions: "Our account of truth is an account of truths in the plural, or processes of leading realized *in rebus,* and having only this quality in common, that they pay." In *Charles S. Peirce,* p. 195, Apel groups James together with Nietzsche as holding the "subjectivistic, fictionalistic, usefulness conception of truth" characteristic of "vulgar Pragmatism."

Apel cites the following passage from Nietzsche's *The Will to Power*, translated by W. Kaufmann and R. J. Hollingdale (New York: Random House, 1967), p. 272: "Truth is the kind of error without which a species of life could not live. The value for life is ultimately decisive."

11. See G. E. Moore, "Professor James' Pragmatism," *Proceedings of the Aristotelian Society*, n.s. 8 (1907–08) and Russell, "Dewey's New Logic" in *the Philosophy of John Dewey*, Vol. I of *The Library of Living Philosophers*, P. Schilpp, ed. (La Salle: Open Court, 1939).

12. John Heil applies the term 'consequentialism' to the view that ties "warranted beliefs to practical reasoning and thus conflates epistemic and practical rationality." Those advocating "nonconsequentialism" hold that justification of beliefs is related "exclusively to epistemic norms." See "Believing What One Ought," *Journal of Philosophy* 80 (1983):752–65. Consequentialist pragmatism seems to be what Nicholas Rescher terms "propositional pragmatism" in *The Primacy of Practice* (Oxford: Blackwell, 1973). For propositional pragmatism, Rescher says, "a proposition is to be accepted...if its adoption is maximally success-producing." In *Methodological Pragmatism* (Oxford: Blackwell, 1977), p. 37 Rescher calls this same position "thesis pragmatism."

13. R. B. Braithwaite, *Scientific Explanation* (Cambridge: Cambridge University Press, 1953), p. 253. See also Abraham Wald, *Statistical Decision Functions*, 2nd ed. (New York: Chelsea, 1971), pp. 2ff.

14. Jack Meiland, "What Ought we to Believe? or the Ethics of Belief Revisited," *American Philosophical Quarterly* 17 (1980):15–24.

15. Heil, "Believing What One Ought."

16. Cf. Kyburg, *Probability and the Logic of Rational Belief*, p. 304: "while values may be taken into account (as they must be) in choosing between actions, and statistical evidence may also be taken into account in choosing between actions, it is an obfuscation of the real issues involved in coming to an agreement about what it is that we have learned and can learn from experience to combine both considerations and call the resulting policy a policy of choosing between *hypotheses*, rather than between actions."

17. Rescher terms this "methodological pragmatism." This version of pragmatism, he says, "asserts that a proposition is to be accepted...if it conforms to an epistemically warranted criterion, and that a criterion is warranted if its adoption as a generic principle for propositional acceptance is maximally success-producing." See *Methodological Pragmatism*, pp. 71, 72.

18. "The Dilemma of Determinism" and "The Will to Believe," both in *The Will to Believe and Other Essays* (1897) (New York: Dover, 1956).

19. See U. T. Place, "Is Consciousness a Brain Process?," *British Journal of Psychology* 147 (1956):44–50 and J. C. C. Smart, "Sensations and Brain Processes," *Philosophical Review* 68 (1959):141–56.

20. For the argument for this functionalist revision see Hilary Putnam, "The Nature of Mental States" in N. Block, ed., *Readings in Philosophy of Psychology* (Cambridge: Harvard University Press, 1980).

Bibliography

Annis, David. "A Contextualist Theory of Epistemic Justification." *American Philosophical Quarterly* 15 (1978):213–19.

Armstrong, David. *Belief, Truth and Knowledge*. Cambridge: Cambridge University Press, 1979.

Audi, Robert. "The Causal Structure of Indirect Justification." *Journal of Philosophy* 80 (1983):398–415.

Austin, J. L. *Philosophical Papers*. Oxford: Clarendon Press, 1961.

Ayer, A. J. *Probability and Evidence*. New York: Columbia University Press, 1950.

———. *The Problem of Knowledge*. Baltimore: Penguin Books, 1956.

———. *The Concept of a Person*. New York: St. Martin's, 1963.

———. *The Origins of Pragmatism*. San Francisco: Freeman and Cooper, 1968.

Barker, John. "What You Don't Know Won't Hurt You?" *American Philosophical Quarterly* 13 (1976):303–8.

Belnap, N. and T. Steele. *The Logic of Questions and Answers*. New Haven: Yale University Press, 1976.

Bolzano, Bernard. *Theory of Science* (1837), translated by R. George. Oxford: Blackwell, 1972.

Braithwaite, R. B. *Scientific Explanation*. Cambridge: Cambridge University Press, 1953.

Carnap, Rudolph. "On the Applications of Inductive Logic." *Philosophy and Phenomenological Research* 8 (1947):133–47.

———. *Logical Foundations of Probability*. Chicago: University of Chicago Press, 1950.

———. *The Continuum of Inductive Methods*. Chicago: University of Chicago Press, 1952.

———. "The Aim of Inductive Logic" in *Logic, Methodology and Philosophy of Science*, E. Nagel, P. Suppes, and A. Tarski, eds. Stanford: Stanford University Press, 1962.

Chisholm, Roderick. *Perceiving*. Ithaca: Cornell University Press, 1957.

Clarke, D. S., Jr. *Deductive Logic*. Carbondale: Southern Illinois University Press, 1974.

———. "On Distinguishing the 'Ought' from the 'Rational'." *Philosophia* 15 (1985):251–70.

———. *Practical Inferences*. London: Routledge and Kegan Paul, 1985.

———. *Principles of Semiotic*. London: Routledge and Kegan Paul, 1987.

Denise, Theodore. "On the Nature of INUS Conditionality." *Analysis* 44 (1984):49–52.

137

Dewey, John. *Logic, The Theory of Inquiry.* New York: Holt, 1938.
Donnellan, Keith. "Speaker Reference, Descriptions, and Anaphora" in *Contemporary Perspectives in the Philosophy of Language,* P. French and H. Wettstein, eds. Minneapolis: University of Minnesota Press, 1979.
Feldman, Richard. "Reliability and Justification." *Monist* 68 (1985):159–74.
Feyerabend, Paul. *Against Method.* Highlands: Humanities, 1975.
Fine, Arthur. "Unnatural Attitudes: Realist and Instrumentalist Attachments to Science." *Mind* 95 (1986):49–79.
Foley, R. and R. Fumerton. "Epistemic Indolence." *Mind* 91 (1982):38–56.
Frankfurt, Harry. "Philosophical Certainty." *Philosophical Review* 71 (1962):303–32.
Gettier, Edmund. "Is Justified True Belief Knowledge?" *Analysis* 23 (1963):121–23.
Goldman, Alvin. "Discrimination and Perceptual Knowledge." *Journal of Philosophy* 73 (1976):771–91.
———. "Epistemics: The Regulative Theory of Cognition." *Journal of Philosophy* 75 (1978):509–23.
———. "A Causal Theory of Knowledge" in *Essays on Knowledge and Justification,* G. Pappas and M. Swain, eds. Ithaca: Cornell University Press, 1978.
———. "What is Justified Belief?" in *Justification and Knowledge,* G. S. Pappas, ed. Dordrecht: D. Reidel, 1979.
———. *Epistemology and Cognition.* Cambridge: Harvard University Press, 1983.
Habermas, Jurgen. *Knowledge and Human Interests* (1968), translated by J. J. Shapiro. Boston: Beacon Press, 1971.
Hanson, N. R. *Patterns of Discovery.* Cambridge: Cambridge University Press, 1962.
Harman, Gilbert. *Thought.* Princeton: Princeton University Press, 1973.
———. "Reasoning and Evidence One Does not Possess" in *Midwest Studies in Philosophy,* Vol. V. Minneapolis: University of Minnesota Press, 1980.
———. *Change in View.* Cambridge: MIT Press, 1986.
Heil, John. "Believing What One Ought." *Journal of Philosophy* 80 (1983):752–65.
Hempel, Carl. "Deductive Nomological vs. Statistical Explanation" in *Minnesota Studies in the Philosophy of Science,* Vol. III, H. Feigl and G. Maxwell, eds. Minneapolis: University of Minnesota Press, 1962.
Hintikka, Jaako. "On a Combined System of Inductive Logic." *Acta Philosophica Fennica* 18 (1965):21–30.
———. "Towards a Theory of Inductive Generalizations," in *Logic, Methodology and Philosophy of Science,* Y. Bar-Hillel, ed. Amsterdam: N. Holland, 1965.
Hume, David. *A Treatise of Human Nature* (1739), L. A. Selby-Bigge, ed. Oxford: Clarendon Press, 1888.
James, William. *Pragmatism.* New York: Longmans and Green, 1907.
———. *The Will to Believe and Other Essays* (1897). New York: Dover, 1956.
Jeffrey, Richard. "Valuation and Acceptance of Scientific Hypotheses." *Philosophy of Science* 23 (1956):237–46.
Johnson, Mark. *The Body and the Mind.* Chicago: University of Chicago Press, 1987.
Keynes, J. M. *A Treatise on Probability.* London: Macmillan, 1921.
Kornblith, Hilary. "Justified Belief and Epistemically Responsible Action." *Philosophical Review* 92 (1983):33–48.

Kripke, Saul. "A Puzzle About Belief" in *Meaning and Use,* A. Margalit, ed. Dordrecht: D. Reidel, 1976.
———. *Naming and Necessity.* Cambridge: Harvard University Press, 1980.
Kyburg, Henry, Jr. "Conjunctivitis" in *Induction, Acceptance and Rational Belief,* M. Swain, ed. Dordrecht: D. Reidel, 1969.
———. *Probability and the Logic of Rational Belief.* Middlebury: Wesleyan University Press, 1961.
———. *Probability and Inductive Logic.* London: Macmillan, 1970.
———. *Epistemology and Inference.* Minneapolis: University of Minnesota Press, 1983.
Lakatos, Imre. "Falsification and the Methodology of Scientific Research Programmes" in *Criticism and the Growth of Knowledge,* Lakatos and A. Musgrave, eds. Cambridge: Cambridge University Press, 1970.
———. "Changes in the Problem of Inductive Logic" in *Philosophical Papers,* Vol. I, J. Worrall and G. Currie, eds. Cambridge: Cambridge University Press, 1978.
Lehrer, Keith. "Knowledge, Truth, and Evidence" in *Knowing: Essays in the Analysis of Knowledge,* M. D. Roth and L. Gallis, eds. New York: Random House, 1970.
———. *Knowledge.* London. Oxford University Press, 1974.
Lehrer, K. and T. Paxson. "Knowledge: Undefeated Justified True Belief" in *Essays on Knowledge and Justification,* G. Pappas and M. Swain, eds. Ithaca: Cornell University Press, 1978.
Levi, Isaac. *Gambling with Truth.* New York: Knopf, 1967.
———. *The Enterprise of Knowledge.* Cambridge: MIT Press, 1980.
———. *Decisions and Revisions.* Cambridge: Cambridge University Press, 1984.
Lewis, C. I. *The Ground and Nature of the Right.* New York: Columbia University Press, 1955.
Lowry, Catherine. "Gettier's Notion of Justification." *Mind* 87 (1978):105–8.
Luce, R. D. and H. Raiffa. *Games and Decisions.* New York: Wiley, 1967.
Lycan, William. "Evidence One Does Not Possess." *Australasian Journal of Philosophy* 55 (1977):114–26.
Mackie, John. *The Cement of the Universe.* Oxford: Clarendon Press, 1974.
Malcom, Norman. "Moore and Ordinary Language" in *The Philosophy of G. E. Moore* in *The Library of Living Philosophers,* Vol. IV, P. Schilpp, ed. La Salle: Open Court, 1942.
———. *Knowledge and Certainty.* Englewood Cliffs: Prentice-Hall, 1962.
Mannison, D. S. " 'Inexplicable Knowledge' Does Not Require Belief." *Philosophical Quarterly* 26 (1976):139–48.
Meiland, Jack. "What Ought we to Believe? or the Ethics of Belief Revisited." *American Philosophical Quarterly* 17 (1980):15–24.
Moore, G. E. "Professor James' Pragmatism." *Proceedings of the Aristotelian Society,* n.s. 8 (1907–1908).
Nagel, Ernest. "Carnap's Theory of Induction" in *The Philosophy of Rudolph Carnap,* Vol. XI of *The Library of Living Philosophers,* P. Schilpp, ed. LaSalle: Open Court, 1963.
Nietzsche, Friedrich. *The Will to Power,* translated by W. Kaufmann and R. J. Hollingdale. New York: Random House, 1967.
Nisbett, R. and L. Ross. *Human Inference.* Englewood Cliffs: Prentice Hall, 1980.
Odegard, Douglas. *Knowledge and Skepticism.* Totowa: Rowman and Littlefield, 1982.

Peirce, Charles. *The Collected Papers of Charles Sanders Peirce,* C. Hartshorne and P. Weiss, eds., 6 vols. Cambridge: Harvard University Press, 1934–1936.
Place, U. T. "Is Consciousness a Brain Process?" *British Journal of Psychology* 147 (1956):44–50.
Plantinga, Alvin. "Epistemic Justification." *Nous* 20 (1986):3–18.
Plato. *Theaetetus* in *The Dialogues of Plato,* translated by B. Jowett. New York: Random House, 1920, Vol. II.
Popper, Karl. *Objective Knowledge.* Oxford: Clarendon Press, 1972.
Putnam, Hilary. "The Analytic and Synthetic" in *Minnesota Studies in the Philosophy of Science,* Vol. III, H. Feigl and G. Maxwell, eds. Minneapolis: University of Minnesota Press, 1962.
———. "Is Semantics Possible?" in *Mind, Language and Reality.* Cambridge: Cambridge University Press, 1975.
———. "The Nature of Mental States" in *Readings in Philosophy of Psychology,* N. Block, ed. Cambridge: Harvard University Press, 1980.
———. *Reason, Truth and History.* Cambridge: Cambridge University Press, 1981.
Quine, W. V. O. and J. S. Ullian. *The Web of Belief.* New York: Random House, 1970.
Radford, Colin. "Knowledge—By Examples." *Analysis* 27 (1966):1–11.
Reichenbach, Hans. *The Theory of Probability,* translated by E. Hutton and M. Reichenbach. Berkeley: University of California Press, 1949.
Rescher, Nicholas. *Primacy of Practice.* Oxford: Blackwell, 1973.
———. *Methodological Pragmatism.* Oxford: Blackwell, 1977.
Ring, Merrill. "Knowledge: The Cessation of Belief." *American Philosophical Quarterly* 14 (1977):51–9.
Rorty, Richard. *Consequences of Pragmatism.* Minneapolis: University of Minnesota Press, 1982.
Rudner, Richard. "The Scientist *Qua* Scientist Makes Value Judgments" *Philosophy of Science* 20 (1953):1–6.
Russell, Bertrand. *The Analysis of Mind.* London: Allen and Unwin, 1921.
———. "Dewey's New Logic" in *The Philosophy of John Dewey,* Vol. I of *The Library of Living Philosophers,* P. Schilpp, ed. La Salle: Open Court, 1939.
Ryle, Gilbert. *The Concept of Mind.* New York: Barnes and Noble, 1949.
Sahlin, Nils-Eric. " 'How to be 100% Certain 99.5% of the Time'." *Journal of Philosophy* 83 (1986):91–111.
Salmon, Wesley. *The Foundations of Scientific Inference.* Pittsburgh: Pittsburgh University Press, 1966.
Savage, Leonard. *The Foundations of Statistics,* 2nd ed. New York: Dover, 1972.
Shope, Robert K. *The Analysis of Knowing.* Princeton: Princeton University Press, 1983.
Smart, J. C. C. "Sensations and Brain Processes." *Philosophical Review,* 68 (1959):141–56.
Smith, E. E. and D. L. Medlin. *Categories and Concepts.* Cambridge: Harvard University Press, 1980.
Stalnaker, Robert. *Inquiry.* Cambridge: MIT Press, 1984.
Stich, Steven. *From Folk Psychology to Cognitive Science.* Cambridge: MIT Press, 1983.
Strawson, P. F. *Logico-Linguistic Papers.* London: Methuen, 1971.
Swain, Michael. "Justification and the Basis of Belief" in *Justification and Knowledge,* G. S. Pappas, ed. Dordrecht: D. Reidel, 1979.
Tversky, A. and D. Kahneman. "Judgment Under Uncertainty: Heuristics and

Biases" in *Judgment Under Uncertainty: Heuristics and Biases,* D. Kahneman, P. Slovic, A. Tversky, eds. Cambridge: Cambridge University Press, 1982.

Ullman-Margalit, Edna. "On Presumption." Journal of Philosophy 80 (1983): 143–63.

Unger, Peter. *Ignorance.* Oxford: Clarendon Press, 1975.

———. *Philosophical Relativity.* Minneapolis: University of Minnesota Press, 1983.

Van Fraasen, Bas. "Salmon on Explanation." *Journal of Philosophy* 82 (1985):639–51.

Von Mises, Richard. *Probability, Statistics, and Truth.* New York: Macmillan, 1957, English translation of *Wahrescheinlichkeit, Statistik, und Wahrkeit,* Berlin, J. Springer, 1928.

Von Wright, G. H. *The Logical Problem of Induction,* 2nd ed. Oxford: Blackwell, 1957.

Wald, Abraham. *Statistical Decision Functions,* 2nd ed. New York: Chelsea, 1971.

Weinstein, M. C. and H. V. Fineberg. *Clinical Decision Analysis.* Philadelphia: W. B. Saunders, 1980.

Will, Frederick. "Generalization and Evidence" in *Philosophical Analysis,* M. Black, ed. Englewood Cliffs: Prentice Hall, 1963.

Williams, Bernard. *Problems of the Self.* Cambridge: Cambridge University Press, 1973.

Wittgenstein, Ludwig. *On Certainty,* translated by D. Paul and G. E. M. Anscombe. New York: Harper, 1969.

Ziff, Paul. *Epistemic Analysis.* Dordrecht: D. Reidel, 1984.

Index of Names

Index